"Neil and Simon have a passi
to the Spirit, and a delight in the presence of God. If I could
recommend one book on worship, this would be it."
  – **Mark Bailey,** Lead Pastor, Trinity Cheltenham, and New Wine
  Leadership Team

"Powerfully written, thoughtfully constructed and theologically
robust. This book is a must!"
  – **Kathryn Scott,** worship leader and songwriter, Causeway
  Vineyard, Northern Ireland, and writer of the song "Hungry"

"I highly recommend this book, not only because of its stellar
commitment to sound doctrine and solid advice, but also
because it comes from a place of deep integrity. Give it a read –
you won't be disappointed!"
  – **David Ruis,** worship leader, author, songwriter and church
  planter, Los Angeles, and writer of the song "I will worship"

"This book has a heart for God and a heart for his people. It is
written out of a deep mature love of God and a passion for the
church."
  – **Nick Drake,** worship pastor, St Paul's Hammersmith,
  London, UK

"A collaboration between an influential worship leader and an
inspirational Bible teacher, this book remarries what has often
been rent asunder – God and worship. Read it! Tell others to do
the same."
  – **Kenny Borthwick,** church leader, and chairman of
  New Wine Scotland

NOW TO HIM

PUTTING CHRIST BACK AT THE CENTRE OF OUR WORSHIP

Neil Bennetts and Simon Ponsonby

MONARCH
BOOKS

Oxford, UK & Grand Rapids, Michigan, USA

First published in the UK in 2011 by Monarch Books
(a publishing imprint of Lion Hudson plc)
Wilkinson House, Jordan Hill Road, Oxford OX2 8DR, England
Tel: +44 (0)1865 302750 Fax: +44 (0)1865 302757
Email: monarch@lionhudson.com
www.lionhudson.com

ISBN 978 0 85721 032 6 (print)
ISBN 978 0 85721 172 9 (epub)
ISBN 978 0 85721 171 2 (Kindle)
ISBN 978 0 85721 173 6 (PDF)

Distributed by:
UK: Marston Book Services, PO Box 269, Abingdon, Oxon, OX14 4YN
USA: Kregel Publications, PO Box 2607, Grand Rapids, Michigan 49501

British Library Cataloguing Data
A catalogue record for this book is available from the British Library.

I would like to dedicate this book to the memory Bob Stuckes, my grandad, an exclusive Brethren preacher, who cried when he preached the Gospel.

Simon Ponsonby

Contents

6. Everything in its Right Place   110
Honouring the holy in worship
– NEIL BENNETTS

7. *Coram Deo* – Living Life to the Face of God   134
The presence and power of God in worship
– NEIL BENNETTS

Acknowledgments

To Mum. This book is dedicated to you and the memory of Dad.

To my amazing family – Susie, Lizzy and Sarah. I love you all incredibly, and love the life we share together. Thank you for letting me do what I do – for all the Sundays we eat late, for all the time spent in caravans and airports and tents in the rain, and for keeping my feet firmly on the ground in everything.

To the Trinity Cheltenham church family. Thank you for bearing with me and letting me lead worship for you for the past 17 years. So many memories, so much fun along the way, and so much more to come.

To the Trinity Cheltenham Worship Team past and present. Too many to mention you all, but what an amazing team. You serve above and beyond.

To Mark and Karen Bailey. Thanks for inviting me to be part of the journey, for sticking by me for so long, for entrusting me with so much, and encouraging me through it all. So many of the words I have written in this book come from your own wisdom and insight.

To Dave and Paula Keeper, Tim and Hils Grew and Gareth Dickinson. We're still all here, we're still all standing, and your friendship is more important than ever.

To Eoghan Heaslip. Thank you for enduring friendship and partnership in so much. It will be so good to have you, Becky and the family down in this part of the world finally.

To Jules Woodbridge and Melody Ball. I can't believe I get the chance to lead worship with you and share in leadership with you both. You are both amazing people – thank you for bringing your life, sparkle and sense of fun into this journey of worship.

To Garry and Jill McCrea. For cold beer, kettle chips, red wine, chocolate, and warm friendly conversation at New Wine each year, and for loving us through it all.

To our extended Cheltenham family – Rich, Kath, Maddie and Bertie Warner. Despite supporting the wrong football team we still love you.

To our extended Norwich family – Chris, Ruth, Jessica, Theo and Luke Lynds. We keep hoping one day we will be able to persuade you to move closer.

To Tom and Sue Kent. Thanks for sharing life with me in Norwich, for helping me buy my first electric piano and for all those Saturdays at Carrow Road during "the glory years".

To David Elkington. That conversation some 27 years ago when you suggested I would go into full time worship ministry even though such a role was almost unheard of at the time turned out to be prophetic. It also saved me from pursuing ordination for which I am more grateful than you could ever know!

To Alistair and Hazel Groves. Yes, I'm still hacking my guitar to bits, quoting Fawlty Towers, and still feel that "I know nothing".

To David Ruis. What an inspiration you are. Full of integrity, full of creativity, full of God. A pretty good combination I reckon.

Kathryn Scott. We love Causeway vineyard – thanks for being so welcoming to us, for leading worship at New Wine and for Alan's visit over here for HeartHead Hands. You are an amazing couple.

Naomi Lippett. Thanks friend for many years leading worship together in Cheltenham, and for staying int touch from Canada. If only I could get Skype working properly we could speak more often.

Nick Drake. Thanks dude for wise words, great songs, and

great worship leadership. You still need a hair cut though.

To Brian Doerksen. Happy memories of a few days spent writing, walking, talking and eating steaks on the patio in BC.

To Scott Underwood. Your words of encouragement that first time at New Wine eleven years ago still stay with me. What are you up to these days?

To John and Anne Coles, Bruce Collins, Kenny Borthwick, David and Mary Pytches, Charlie and Anita Cleverly. Great leaders, great wisdom, great inspiration. Thank You.

To Simon Ponsonby. Thanks for letting me hang out with you, for believing in me for this project, and for telling it like it is. You are a huge gift to the Church, to me, and to so many others – keep on going friend.

To Sam, Susie, Jemima, Sarah, Dave, Jimmy, Sophie, Jamie, Gareth, Paul, Rob, Emma, Tom. Thanks for letting me be part of your own journey in worship leadership. It has been a joy to share a little bit of life with you. The next generation will be fortunate to have you leading them.

Neil Bennetts

Foreword

An article objecting to new trends in church music appeared in an American newspaper saying,

> There are several reasons for opposing it. One, it's too new. Two, it's often worldly, even blasphemous. The new Christian music is not as pleasant as the more established style. Because there are so many new songs, you can't learn them all. It puts too much emphasis on instrumental music rather than godly lyrics. This new music creates disturbances making people act indecently and disorderly. The preceding generation got along without it. It's a money making scam and some of these new music upstarts are lewd and loose.

You may find yourself agreeing or sympathizing with this critique of modern church music. A particular worship leader or church may even come to mind. This article, however, was written in 1723 in opposition to Isaac Watts, the writer of "When I Survey The Wondrous Cross". Over the years the church has spent much time arguing and dividing over the subject of worship. It is always a tragedy when worship is misunderstood and simply reduced to a style or genre of music. People will always have opinions and preferences when it comes to the corporate expression of worship, but as God's people we continually need to shift our gaze from the mechanics of worship to the object of worship; the Lord Jesus Christ.

Now to Him draws us back to the heart of worship, allowing us to move beyond songs, liturgies and styles. Worship is about relationship. It is our wholehearted response to God's extravagant love and great glory. This response affects everything we are and everything we will ever be. Worship is the total alignment of our heart, soul, mind and strength with the will of God. It is the activity and purpose we were created for. Our beginning and our end.

The impact of genuine and true worship should never be underestimated. This is not a side issue. I genuinely believe that if we want to see the transformation of ourselves, our churches and our society, then the key will be understanding all that it means to be worshippers of God. The great Archbishop William Temple wrote, "This world can be saved from political chaos and collapse by one thing, and that is worship." This book is not simply for a select group of worship leaders or musicians. This is an important read for anyone passionate to see a fresh move of God.

Now to Him is a wonderful blend of theological, biblical inspiration, twinned with a practical and challenging critique of where we can grow and develop in the area of worship. Over the years the teaching and ministry of both Simon Ponsonby and Neil Bennetts have impacted me. Simon teaches with a passion and vulnerability that reaches straight to the heart, leaving you with a profound sense of the mystery of God's love and grace. This book is no different. As I read through the pages my heart was awakened once again to the glory, majesty and mercy of Christ. As Simon writes he beautifully conveys the sheer privilege and joy it is to be known and to know the Creator of the heavens and earth. Neil is thoughtful and has been actively involved leading worship and training others for many years. He is a man of integrity and cares passionately about the local church. His reflections and insights into the specifics of leading worship through music and song are golden. He asks the difficult questions, he probes, challenges and brings to the forefront essential issues that need careful consideration: Where is worship going? Who is it for? What are we missing?

This book is gloriously Christ-centric, renewing a sense of wonder and awe that feeds the mind and inspires the soul. It will help you to worship with understanding and ultimately leave your hearts full of praise and adoration for the God who alone is able.

Tim Hughes

Chapter 1

Worship

THE BIBLICAL CHARACTER AND CULTURE OF WORSHIP

Simon Ponsonby

Augustine of Hippo (AD 354–430) is perhaps the greatest theologian of the Western church. He fought against heresies on several fronts; he articulated the great doctrines of the church in grand architectonic fashion to the glory of God. He is often quoted, from his autobiographical work *Confessions*, as expressing the innate human longing for God: "you have made us for yourself and our heart is restless till it finds its rest in you."

What is less well known is that this very statement, which defines human identity in terms of innate orientation towards God that is only able to find its fulfilment in God, is found in his reflection on worship:

> Great are you, O Lord, and worthy of high praise.
> Great is your strength and of your wisdom there is no
> counting. Even man is, in his own way, a part of your
> creation, and longs to praise you... You stir us up to
> take delight in your praise; for you have made us for
> yourself and our heart is restless till it finds its rest in
> you.[1]

For Augustine, to be a human is to long for God – a longing fulfilled only in the act of worshipping God. One cannot be fully human if one doesn't worship God.

---

1 *Confessions* 1:1.

The prophet Isaiah declared that we were created to praise God.[2] Saint Paul thrilled at the thought that we were adopted and redeemed to praise and glorify God.[3] Paul wrote that the archetypical sin was to withhold worship and glory from God, and to offer worship elsewhere to created things, to idols.[4] The vision John the Beloved gives us of heaven is bursting with worship and the very songs that are sung around the throne declare God worthy of worship by all he created.[5] The Protestant tradition picks up these themes and in the famous statement of faith, the Westminster Catechism, declares that "we are created to give glory to God". In the twentieth century, C. S. Lewis (and, in similar vein, John Piper) mused over this theme of being created to worship and wondered, even worried, whether it suggested God's sole purpose in creating us was to have sycophants.

But Lewis rightly saw that in our worship, in our giving to God, we receive – we are actualized, we become who we are, we are fulfilled:

> I think we delight to praise what we enjoy because the praise not merely expresses but completes the enjoyment; it is its appointed consummation. It is not out of compliment that lovers keep on telling one another how beautiful they are; the delight is incomplete till it is expressed. It is frustrating to have discovered a new author and not to be able to tell anyone how good he is; to come suddenly, at the turn of the road, upon some mountain valley of unexpected grandeur and then to have to keep silent because the people with you care for it no more than for a tin can in the ditch; to hear a good joke and find no one to share it with... If it were possible for a created soul fully... to "appreciate", that is to love and delight in, the worthiest object of all, and simultaneously at every

2   Isaiah 43:7.
3   Ephesians 1:3–14.
4   Romans 1:18–25.
5   Revelation 4:11.

moment to give this delight perfect expression, then that soul would be in supreme beatitude... To see what the doctrine really means, we must suppose ourselves to be in perfect love with God – drunk with, drowned in, dissolved by, that delight which, far from remaining pent up within ourselves as incommunicable, hence hardly tolerable, bliss, flows out from us incessantly again in effortless and perfect expression; our joy is no more separable from the praise in which it liberates and utters itself than the brightness a mirror receives is separable from the brightness it sheds. The Scotch catechism says that man's chief end is "to glorify God and enjoy Him forever." But we shall then know that these are the same thing. Fully to enjoy is to glorify. In commanding us to glorify Him, God is inviting us to enjoy Him.[6]

The culture of worship

God's first commandment, given through Moses to the people of Israel, is about worship.

Exclusive, God-giving worship:

I am the Lord your God, who brought you out of the land of Egypt, out of the house of slavery. You shall have no other gods before me. You shall not make for yourself a carved image, or any likeness of anything... You shall not bow down to them or serve them, for I the Lord your God am a jealous God.[7]

This worship is God's due, for He alone is God, He alone is the deliverer. But the fact that He had to give this commandment shows that He knows the tendency of the human heart to worship

---

6   "The Problem of Praise in the Psalms", in *Reflections on the Psalms*, New York: Harcourt, Brace and World, 1958, pp. 90–98.
7   Exodus 20:2–5.

just about everything other than God. We are made to worship God – we are saved to worship God, but as St Paul highlights in Romans 1:18–25, we will often choose to worship the created over the Creator, inanimate things rather than the very source of life. We create idols and bow down before them – an idol being anything we substitute for God.

As Augustine above said, we are all born worshippers. The issue is never whether we worship but what. In Oxford, where I live, often God is replaced by gods of intellect, the mind, academic success. The biggest and best brain is worshipped. We have the high priestly hierarchy of dons, fellows and professors and their vestments of hood and gown, and we have their religious ceremonies of initiation, matriculation, confirmation, examination, and graduation.

In the suburbs, millions get up on Sunday and worship by going to car boot sales, or washing their Mondeos or BMWs or 4x4s. Audi once had an advert for their Cabriolet which simply stated, "Worship here". The new cathedrals are our shopping centres or the giant out-of-town shopping malls where millions go on pilgrimage and offer homage at the altars of the tills. On Christmas Day 2007, more people in the UK bought online than attended church!

In 1998, billions were glued to their TVs watching the football World Cup. At the cathedrals (stadiums) the high priests (players) gave offerings (goals) on the altars (nets), with churchwardens (referees) in attendance. At the inauguration of that World Cup in France, a little girl read a poem entitled "Take us to a better place".

Millions cheered, or were in tears!

Worship!

The music on the BBC to accompany the 2006 football World Cup was the tune to the hymn "Thine be the glory, risen, conquering Son". Was this not close to blasphemy – attributing to a game what belongs to God alone?

The character of biblical worship

Romans 12:1 indicates that worship is a way of life – rather than just the songs we sing in a church! Paul wants the believers to offer every aspect of their lives to God – in particular stressing holy living. Many people are quick to sing on Sunday and sin on Monday. But "worship" is our "walk" with God. Whatever we do, we do as unto the Lord. Whenever we step out in faith or sacrifice the flesh, we are worshipping – offering ourselves as a sacrifice to God.

In Scripture, however, the normative understanding of praise and worship words (occurring about 400 times) reflects speech expressing adoration, blessing, and honour. Our word "worship" is from the Old English "worth-scipe", meaning to give or declare something or someone's worth, to give value.

Other words in the original biblical languages that are translated into English generally as "worship" or "praise" include:

- **Old Testament Hebrew:** *segad* (bow down), *abad* (serve), *shacah* (bow), *halal* (bless), *yadah* (praise; from the root *yad* = hand).
- **New Testament Greek:** *doxazo* (glorify), *eusebeo* (revere), *proskuneo* (bow/kiss), *latreo* (serve).

These convey a demonstrative aspect to worship alongside the vocal aspect.

The right response of creature to Creator (Psalm 95)

Worship is a recognition of who God is as Lord, Saviour, Master, King, and Ruler.

We worship at God's footstool, we worship at His feet, we acknowledge our dependence and creatureliness, we humble ourselves, and we honour God. But even as we humble ourselves before God, we are also aware that we meet Him as the beloved before our divine lover. The psalmist understood this; hence his constant worship refrain, "his steadfast love endures forever".[8]

Worship can be the whispers between lovers, an intimate expression of affection.

The splendid obsession of heaven

Worship is the preoccupation of eternity.

Whatever else we do, however else we will be occupied, in heaven there will be joyful, spontaneous, overflowing, uninhibited delighting in God. Revelation 4 shows the saints laying their crowns before Him and falling down. The Greek is iterative, a present continuous action of constantly laying down crowns and laying down ourselves before the throne. In order for this to occur, the Lord must constantly raise us up and crown us each time. What incredible extravagant grace! God gives us the very gifts we worship Him with.

The response to revelation

Those who worship little, understand little.

As we study God's word, understand His character, and experience His goodness, worship becomes our automatic response. The medieval saint, Julian of Norwich, would shout out loud praises to God in Latin after reading her Bible. John and Elaine Beekman went as missionaries to the Chol Indians in Mexico. After faithful sacrificial service for twenty-five years, there were 12,000 converts. Interestingly, when they arrived, no one ever sang; there were no songs, no singing in the Chol tribe's tradition. They didn't even have a word for "sing" in their vocabulary.

But when they were converted, when they were Spirit-filled, they began singing praises to God, so much so that they invented a new word and changed their name to become the "singing tribe".

---

8   Psalms 106:1; 107:1; 118:1; 136:1.

The goal of our salvation

We are elected, chosen, redeemed and sealed, all to the praise of God's glorious Grace.[9] But as C. S. Lewis points out, this is not because God desires sycophants, though worship is God's due; it also restores our fallenness and fulfils our humanity – it's what we were made for.

Paul in Romans 1:18–24 says that we were created to know and worship God. In turning away and worshipping idols, we lose the glory that God gave us as beings created in His image. Worship glorifies God but it also restores us to our right glory. When we worship, we become authentic, whole. The converse is also true, as Peter Shaffer said in his play *Equus*: "If you don't worship, you shrink."

The conflict over worship

Jewish Tradition says that the devil was once an archangel who stood before God and conducted the worship being offered to God. Rather than being content with his role as a choir conductor, a conduit of worship, he became proud (beware, worship leaders!) and desired to draw that praise and worship to himself. And God threw him and the angels that adored him out of His presence. Ever since, Satan has continued to deviate worship from God to himself. Even as God was giving the first commandment – to have no idols and to worship no gods but Yahweh – the devil was at work in Israel's camp, causing them to create a golden bull-calf idol, worshipping it and engaging in licentious behaviour.

Idolatry and immorality have always gone hand in hand.

Paul clearly links the two in Romans 1, as if summing up Israel's history, where they worshipped the pagan gods Baal and Ashtoreth and indulged in the indecent sexual expression associated with these fertility gods.

Satan seeks to rob God of His due, and he seeks to corrupt

---

9   Ephesians 1:6, 11, 14.

humanity in their duty. Paul writes that behind every idol is a demon.[10] All worship not given to God in Christ Jesus is worship that the evil one draws to himself. In Revelation 13, St John records that a key mark of the personified antichrist is robbing God of His worship and drawing worship to an image of the beast!

Long ago God said to Pharaoh: "Let my people go, that they may serve me", but Pharaoh resisted, wanting to keep them to worship him by their subservient work, building buildings to his glory, not God's.

Satan has always resisted the worship of God in Christ Jesus. Satan sought to deflect worship from Christ at His birth.[11] The Magi went to Herod and said, "Where is he who has been born king of the Jews? For we... have come to worship him." Herod, demonically inspired, tried to have Christ killed rather than worshipped.

Satan sought to deflect worship from Christ after His baptism.[12] Having been declared the Son of God, Jesus is tested by Satan and the climax of the tests is: "Worship me, and all this I will give you." The devil is trying to buy true worship. Jesus rebukes him, saying, "It is written, worship God, and serve Him only."

Satan sought to deflect worship from Christ at his triumphal entry, when the Pharisees were incensed at the worship being offered to Jesus, and told Him to rebuke the disciples for singing hallelujahs.

Elsewhere the term "rebuke", meaning "to muzzle", was used by Jesus against the demons – but here the demonic wanted to silence the worship. Jesus replied that the very stones would cry out if they tried to stop the praise.

In the early church, one major reason why the authorities persecuted and killed Christians was because of their "exclusive

---

10 1 Corinthians 10:20.
11 Matthew 2.
12 Matthew 4.

worship of Jesus". The Romans would accept Jesus as a god within their pantheon, if Christians also worshipped the emperor, but the exclusive worship of one God, Jesus, was to be exterminated.

Today, in church, the battlefield is often focused on the worship, and often on the mind of the worshipper. How many times has our mind been distracted from worshipping God to thinking about anything but God – the person in front, the lunch, ourselves. John Donne, the English poet, once observed: 'I throw myself down in my chamber, and I call in and invite God and his angels thither, and when they are there, I neglect God and his angels for the noise of a fly, for the rattling of a coach, for the whining of a door.' The enemy wages war in every church over the worship; ask any pastor where the greatest area of criticism and conflict is, and it will invariably be centred around worship, and then finance, which is itself a form of worship. The enemy always takes a great interest in influencing the worship group, or the choir.

I remember ministering at a church weekend. My worship leader pulled out at the last minute; the rector challenged me over my choice of songs for the guest service; the choir were at loggerheads with the rector, utterly independent, insisted on robing and processing in at an evangelistic event, and sitting in their choir stalls, even though they had no part in the special service. Then the curate told me later that two members of the choir were having an illicit affair. The war for worship was also seen when I was speaking at a university chapel; afterwards, at supper, the choir discussed obscene sex acts! A year later I was invited back and the set lectionary reading was about the Pharisees; the text was: "this people honours me with their lips, but their heart is far from me".[13] I preached strongly and faithfully on the passage, but days later I received a sharp rebuke from the chaplain. The choir had complained to him, rather than being convicted by my sermon.

13 Matthew 15:8.

The climax of worship

The most important thing we must grasp is that worship is about giving to God – it's for *His* benefit, not ours. Nevertheless, when we worship and praise, we are blessed also. We have already noted that in worship, as we give God glory, we receive glory, we are restored in our glory, *imago dei*. To worship is to be humanized, glorified. Furthermore, whenever we worship and praise, God comes.

Consider Psalm 22:3, where God is said to be "enthroned on the praises of his people". This is the same idea that we find in 1 Samuel 4:4 and Exodus 25:22, which speak of God inhabiting (being enthroned above) the ark of the covenant. When we praise God, God draws near. Worship woos Him, it intensifies His presence, making more of the God who is with us; and when God is present, He is present in power and glory.

When the twelve tribes of Israel marched out, Judah (meaning "praise") led the way (Numbers 12); and as they marched forward in worship, they were victorious over their enemies. Jehoshaphat defeated Moab by placing a worship team at the front of the army.[14] When we worship, strongholds are broken and dark chains are released. It is precisely because worship is so powerful, because it is liberating, that the evil one opposes it so tenaciously. Martin Luther rightly noted, "The Devil hates a singing Christian."

Merlin Carothers wrote a powerful book entitled *From Prison to Praise* in which he showed how the life of worship transforms the believer, delivering them from self-pity and fears and strongholds, and putting them in the presence of God, of faith, of blessing.

When we worship, we encounter God. When we encounter God, we meet the one who can heal, deliver, save, bless. I suspect we could greatly reduce the hours spent in counselling, ministering and praying with and for those in our churches who

14 1 Chronicles 20:22.

are struggling, if only we could get them worshipping – turning their attention from themselves to God, entering His presence, experiencing His power. The Scottish saint, Robert Murray McCheyne, used to argue that for every one look at ourselves in our sin, problems and struggles, we should take ten looks at Christ.

The power of God to heal released in worship

I have occasionally heard stories of God's power coming down on a congregation in worship and healing and deliverance. I want to finish this chapter by quoting the testimony of a woman who was severely disabled, but who was remarkably healed during worship at a meeting I was at. I spoke to the doctor who interviewed her immediately following this and who believed it a miracle, and I have spoken to close friends of the lady and, a year later, the lady herself, who had kept her healing. What stands out is that God spoke to her, and she was healed in worship – not during prayer ministry.

> In February 2001 I had a stroke followed by a couple of TIAs or mini strokes. During that time we moved from Bolton to St Budeaux in Plymouth where, for the next few years, I underwent tests under a consultant neurologist at Derriford hospital. In March of 2007 I was diagnosed with a brain tumour. I underwent a form of radiotherapy called stereostatic radiotherapy which involves being fitted into a "halo" which enables the radiotherapist to fix your head to the table whilst the radiotherapy takes place; the treatment means that you receive all the radiotherapy all at once instead of over a period of time. Quite traumatic. Almost immediately we discovered that the treatment had done some damage. My vestibular nerve had

been badly damaged and so my balance began to deteriorate. Two consultants got together to decide what to do – a neurosurgeon/consultant and an ENT consultant who specializes in balance problems. The ENT man proposed an operation of about ten hours in length where the pair of them would work together to remove the now dead tumour, the vestibular nerve and all the workings of my inner ear. However, the neuro man said it would be too risky a procedure due to my stroke history. He proposed to leave things as they were for another twelve months to see if things would improve, even though week by week I was getting steadily worse... Praise the Lord for that decision!

I came to New Wine excited – we had brought thirty of our church family with us – and amazingly not even thinking of a healing. By now I was using a stick around the house, a three-wheeled walker during the day, and by around 4 p.m. I had to resort to a wheelchair. I hadn't been out of the house without a minder for four years and had really become a recluse, shunning company and stepping out of ministry – you do rather become a target for the healing ministry, and not always in the most helpful and sensitive of ways. So to be frank, I was all healed out and had come to sigh deeply when the next person came along to lay hands on me. I had no expectation of being healed, yet knew I was completely loved by God and was calmly trusting Him for my future. I actually felt that I didn't need to be healed to be a whole person. At the same time I was in a terrible spiritual desert place. I was being held up by the faithful prayers of others so had only the briefest of conversations with God – my stomach would literally drop at the thought of reading my Bible.

I sat through the worship in my wheelchair –

singing rather than praising. If I did raise my arms, I rested them on the arms of my wheelchair, half-heartedly going through the motions.

Then Heidi Baker's indescribable opening to her preach: in the first few seconds I thought, "What an incredible voice…" Then it was as if the doors of heaven had opened and Jesus Himself was standing amongst us, thrilled by our worship and radiating love for and to us. What an incredible evening! Still, amazingly, I went back to the caravan without any desire to be healed, not even for one second thinking about it; it never occurred to me even to ask for it. I did know, however, that I did have to deal with the "desert place". Greg Haslam's talks were immensely helpful, as was the sensitive, gentle and incredibly wise counsel I received from the couple in the pastoral care centre.

And so to Friday evening! Again I was singing rather than praising in my wheelchair. When the line "You heal all my disease" came (I never sang that particular line), I fleetingly thought, "You've not healed mine!" But I always sing "I trust in you, I trust in you". Immediately I felt a power pass through me from the top of my head to my toes, and with it came complete and utter certainty without doubt. I'm healed. Seconds later I heard the audible voice of God say, "If you want to go to the front and dance, you can!" I replied, "No thanks, I'd like to sit here for a moment; hope you don't mind!" I leaned over to Stephen my husband and said, "Stephen, I'm healed!" to which he replied, "Oh, right." Those who know Stephen know that he is so laid back he is horizontal, but is a deeply godly man, and his "Oh, right" was the "Amen" to years of faithful prayer and longing.

So, there I sat all through Simon Ponsonby's

pertinent preach. He asked in conclusion for people who felt that they were in the desert place to kneel to be prayed for. I asked Stephen to help me out of the wheelchair so that I could kneel whilst a lovely lady prayed for me. I remained sitting on the floor for a while until I badly needed to use the ladies'! I also knew that I had to walk there unaided, so I got off the floor, on my own, stood for a moment to test my legs, on my own, and then walked round, over and through the crowd out into the very uneven roadway, up steps, down steps and back into the meeting, every step a miracle. Only to be met at the door by two very amazed people who had prayed for me on the previous day. At no point had I asked for healing or to my knowledge been prayed for, for this specific healing. God arrived in the atmosphere of praise and worship and chose to lift me to my feet. I spoke to a doctor at the front of the stage who gave Mark Bailey the thumbs up, and the next thing I knew, I was up the steps (unaided) and onto the stage.

On returning, on foot, to the campsite, my church family were all seated in a circle waiting for me; they had decorated our caravan with streamers, Chinese lanterns and candles. There in the centre was my wheelchair, all folded away and completely wrapped up. It went straight into the boot of the car, not to be used since.

I danced my way through worship on the last evening after walking from venue to venue all day, released, loved and protected. Praise the Lord!

We are created as worshippers. If we don't worship God, we will find some other object for our innate impulse to worship.

When we worship God, God comes – and when He comes

He restores, heals, delivers, graces.

It is because worship is God's due, and our destiny, that worship is so contested by the world, the flesh and the devil.

Throughout this book, we will continue to explore the nature of worship, the obstacles to worship, the rewards of worship, and the one we worship.

Chapter 2

The Kingdom of Grace

GOD COURTING THE AFFECTION OF HIS WORLD

Neil Bennetts

I am father to two beautiful girls, Lizzy and Sarah. Although this is not without challenges, I love being a father to my daughters. And this stage in their lives is especially wonderful. They are at that age where they are mature enough to have great fun and conversations with, and still innocent enough not to be causing me too much stress. I am sure that will change over time, and like any father, I am aware that probably at some point they will do things which I won't approve of, and that may cause me some pain. But I reckon that they could do anything – absolutely anything – and I will not love them any less. I reckon that if they turn up at our back door after adventures that lead them to awful places in the company of awful people, I will still be desperate to embrace them.

Of course, I do hope that I will be an important voice in their lives, and that I will be able to instil good values and theology in them. I hope they will do well in their studies and get good jobs. I hope they will find good husbands and raise great families. Of course I have such dreams and aspirations for them. But however much they may depart from the good and true way of life that I dream for them, I think that in me – for them – it will always be grace that will win the day.

Maybe I haven't been hurt enough yet by them, or disappointed enough by what they get involved with at this stage, but I don't think that I will be able to catch the glint in Lizzy's eyes and not find that I have grace there for her. I don't think I will ever be able to see that little frown on Sarah's forehead and not want to shower her with all the love in the world, whatever her world looks like at the time, or the journey that has taken her there.

Despite the fact that at some time or another it will probably cause me to lay aside any sense of logic, predictability or reason, I believe that in me – for them – grace will always triumph.

Of course I am wise enough in the ways of the world to know that, unfortunately, every father is not like that, and I'm really thankful to God that it comes naturally for me. I hope I will always be this way. I can't really imagine that I won't be. But whereas I may most easily operate in grace where my daughters are concerned, I am also equally aware that, more generally than not, I am most comfortable operating in life – whether work or ministry or home life – with something that is more regimented, more organized, more rational, more predictable and more deserving than grace seems to require of me. I prefer a defined set of inputs, designed to give a predictable result. Grace is generally just a little bit too messy for me.

Defined inputs, with a predictable outcome. That's my comfort zone. That's my love language. And although you may laugh at me (and many people do – a lot of the time, as it happens), I reckon that many of us would prefer to operate in this sort of way. For many of us, operating with a set of rules and regulations with predefined causes and effects is actually easier than operating with anything more messy, like grace. It's far easier to have rules for life that you can plug into and know what the outcome will be. It's less demanding on our time. It's less demanding on our prayer life or our faith. And it's far less risky.

The trouble is, it seems that God above all seems to view life through a lens of grace, and if you are like me, that challenges such preferences. In fact, it turns them upside down. But the truth of the matter is that we are part of a Kingdom of Grace, where grace – the unmerited, undeserved, unabating, unrationed, unrelenting, irrational favour of God – will win the day.

And it is with this grace that God has courted, continues to court, and will continue to court for the rest of eternity, the affections of His world.

Courting the affection of His world: The biblical narrative of grace

Grace weaves its way through the whole of the Bible because grace has always been in the nature of God, and that nature never changes. In Genesis the place of intimacy and closeness with God that we were created to enjoy gave way, through sin, to a place of separation from God. Very quickly God's people moved from paradise to desert, from joyful sonship to arrogant self-interest, from blessed togetherness and harmony to insecurity, corruption and murder.[15] A flood and a righteous man called Noah became key parts of God's plan for restoration. Noah was saved, by grace, from the flood, and his descendants repopulated the earth, but very soon, grace became a distant memory and God's people slipped back into the ways of idolatry. The result was that the people whom God had created for worship and community were scattered to the far corners of the world in confusion and disgrace and separation from their Creator.[16]

God then called Abraham to be His servant, His means of grace to once again restore our relationship with Him. Through Abraham, God's intention was to restore all people to Himself once more. Abraham was chosen to lead the people of God, a holy nation who would be God's people here on earth, to worship Him and serve Him. Abraham was chosen that all people on the

15 Genesis 6.
16 Genesis 11:9.

earth would be blessed through the people of God,[17] but the people of God lost their way again and went on another journey away from the things of God and ended up in slavery in Egypt.

Moses was another person who was chosen to be the means by which God showed His grace again. Moses led the people of God out of slavery. He was the one to whom the law was given on Mount Sinai, and to whom God showed His grace.[18] We probably know the story, how God's people rebelled again against God's initiatives of grace. We know how the people that God chose to be His instruments of grace on earth became rebellious and self-absorbed and arrogant once more.

So by the time Jesus came to earth, we find the people of God in a total mess, entrenched in their religious ways, with their true purpose in life pretty much abandoned. As the people of God, they had been chosen by grace to be instruments of that grace to all the people of the earth, chosen by God to reveal the ways and purposes of God to all people, chosen by God to live in closeness to Him. Although repeatedly subject to God's onslaught of grace, their continual disobedience had led them to become a people separate from the God they should have been close to, and detached from the world they were intended to reach.

And as so often happens in such circumstances, when relationship breaks down, more and more process and procedure and religion takes its place. The people of God constructed religious, social and ethnic barriers in life that they used to determine people's worth and standing not only before fellow men, but before God Himself. Never in the history of man had there ever been a stronger sense that in terms of God and His Kingdom, you were either on the inside or the outside. Even in the temple itself – the place where there should have been more evidence and understanding of community and purpose than anywhere else – there was a sign that hung on the wall at the entrance to the inner courts that effectively

---

17 Genesis 12:3.
18 Exodus 33:12.

barred Gentiles from entering.

The disease of un-grace had made its way right to the spiritual heart of God's people.

It was into this environment that Jesus came and spoke His own grace-message.

A fresh announcement of grace: Jesus' message of grace to a world living with un-grace

In Matthew 5, when Jesus spoke on the mountain in the words that we know as the Sermon on the Mount, He spoke them to a large crowd of people from Galilee, the Decapolis, Jerusalem, Judea and the region across the Jordan.

The ten Greek cities that made up the Decapolis were under Roman occupation, and the Romans had rebuilt those cities one by one, building temples within them that were designed for the worship of the emperor. Their citizens were largely non-Jewish. They were the ceremonially unclean, the unholy. In all likelihood they had never read the Jewish Scriptures, had no idea who Jesus really was, and did not understand the concept of a Messiah. Many of them, as they yielded to the pressure of the occupying Romans and their requirement for worshipping their emperor, would have been idolaters.

They were on the outside.

And on this day, on a mountainside in Galilee, they stood alongside the Jews.

The Jews were on the inside.

They were on the inside because they had been born to the right parents at the right time in the right place. They were the "right'r'us". They were descendants of Abraham. The chosen ones. The ones who knew about God, and read the Scriptures and were allowed to go to the temple to worship. They would have had a concept of the Messiah. They may even have heard about Jesus reading the scroll in the synagogue in Nazareth, where He declared Himself as such.[19]

So on that day, on a mountain in Galilee, those on the inside gathered alongside those on the outside and they waited to hear what Jesus would say. They had followed him around for a while now. They had seen people healed. A paralytic dropped through the roof of a house where Jesus taught had got up and walked. A man with leprosy had been cleansed. Change was in the air and they were probably desperate to hear what on earth was causing it.

In fact this gathering on the mountainside was probably the largest and most diverse gathering in that generation.[20] Not only were the first disciples there, but amongst them that day would have been the tax collectors, the prostitutes, the social outcasts, the lepers, the lowest of the low. As well as the religious chosen ones from Jerusalem, Judea, and Galilee, amongst the crowd there would have been some of the most broken and despised people around. They were all probably as much sceptical as they were intrigued as they stood there waiting.

But by the end of this sermon, the whole crowd would be amazed.[21]

As they stand there, Jesus finally stands up before them and speaks, and He announces that the Kingdom of Grace is for all of them. Regardless of what their world looked like at that moment. Regardless of the journey that had brought them to that point. All those people – from so many tribes and tongues and nations and ethnic backgrounds and social statuses – Jesus described them all as blessed. They were blessed not because of anything they had done to deserve it. They were blessed because the Kingdom of Grace was for them. All of them.

---

19 Luke 4:18.
20 Many people have their own view as to whom Jesus was addressing in the Sermon on the Mount. It is the disciples who are mentioned at the outset, but the whole crowd was impacted by the end. I am of the view that, whether Jesus directed it primarily at the disciples or not, this message was intended for everyone.
21 Matthew 7:28.

He said that this was a new day – of grace.

That this was a new season – of grace.

That this was a new age – of grace.

And He said that things were going to be different from now on.

He said that from now on, it was not going to be their ethnic background, their bloodline, their physical well-being or social status that determined their worth before God. He said that from now on, their worth before God was not going to be dependent on who they were, but on who He was.

He said that wherever they came from and whatever broken heap of a mess they found themselves in, they were to count themselves as blessed.

Blessed.

Happy.

Because the Kingdom of Grace was for them.

In these moments Jesus was not giving instructions.[22] He was not telling this diverse rabble of people what they had to do to qualify for His favour. He was not giving them another set of laws to follow, another set of rituals to perform.

He was telling them that the Kingdom was there for them.

That God was there for them.

That God was near to them.

In fact not only near to them, but right there beside them.

And because of that, things were going to be very, very different from now on.

The poor, the oppressed, the outcasts, the prostitutes, the walked-over, the physically broken, the sexually confused were finding out that the Kingdom of Grace was for them, just as much as it was for the well-off, the socially acceptable, the athletic, and the ritually pure.

---

22 Fredrick Dale Bruner says: "The beatitudes must first be heard as grace, or they will not be heard correctly. Jesus' beatitudes are first sheer gifts" (*The Christbook*, Wm B. Eerdmans Publishing, 2004, p. 156). He goes on to say: "The beatitudes are the overture to Jesus' Sermon Symphony... they are the most significant words ever spoken: their simplicity is deceptive. There is gold under this ground."

In fact Jesus was saying that in this Kingdom of Grace, people who had done nothing to earn it would get to be people they had no right to be and that they would get to do things that they had done nothing to deserve. Or as Rob Bell puts it:

> Blessed are the losers, those at the end of their rope, the spiritual zeros, the bankrupt, pathetic, lame, the out of it, those without a trace of good, the morally empty, the pathetic. Blessed are the quiet ones, the shy ones, the unnoticed, the wall flowers, the average. Blessed are those who live with a deep nagging sense that life is passing them by, that they aren't getting their slice of the pie, that they aren't in some profound way keeping up. Blessed are those who can't seem to get it all together, who can't seem to get on top of things, who constantly feel like they fall short, because God's world has plenty of room for them.[23]

And as the Jesus-on-earth section of the biblical grace narrative unfolds, we find that this Kingdom of Grace would be one where a corrupt financier would become the friend of the King, an evil murderer would become one of the most significant writers in the Bible and a destitute prostitute would be held up as an example of a true worshipper to all future generations.

Blows your mind, doesn't it?

A corrupt financier getting to be pally with the Saviour.

A murderer getting to be a church leader.

A prostitute getting to show us about worship.

I wonder if this would ever happen in my church.

Or your church.

But it was happening then.

It was so very different to what had gone before.

But of course, this was the new day, the new season, the new age of grace.

---

23 Rob Bell did a sermon series at Mars Hill on the Sermon on the Mount in 2009–2010

Grace changes everything: The life-transforming power of grace

No wonder that this message of grace even confounded the great biblical teachers of the day. Nicodemus was one of the most prominent teachers of Israel. He was one of the most inside of insiders. When Jesus tried to tell him about this Kingdom of Grace, he just couldn't get his head round it. Jesus told him that the things of the Kingdom were for anyone who was willing just to receive it as a gift from heaven.[24] Nicodemus was a Pharisee. He knew how things had been done in the past. He knew the rituals and processes that had to be undertaken to qualify, to get on the inside. He knew such things, understood such things, embodied such things, lived such things, and taught such things. Now here was Jesus, the person who had come, hopefully, to affirm such things, blowing it all apart. Jesus told him that the Kingdom of Grace was for whosoever decided to received it, regardless of background. Suddenly Nicodemus realized that he knew nothing.

Then Jesus met a Roman centurion in Capernaum.[25] His servant was sick at home and he wanted Jesus to heal him. This was a Roman. One of the oppressors in the land. One of the people who were forcing the inhabitants of the land to bow down and worship the emperor. Someone who was using power and status and privilege and military might to persecute people. His servant was ill and he wanted Jesus to heal him.

His servant.

So he was not only a Roman, but he was someone who employed slave labour in his home. He was an oppressor of freedom and rights and an employer of slave labour. If there was anyone who was completely undeserving of the things of the Kingdom, it was him. He was one of the most outside of outsiders.

---

24 John 3:1–21.
25 Matthew 8:5–13.

In fact it seems like even he suspected that.[26] But maybe he had been on that mountainside that day some time ago, listening to Jesus speak. Maybe he had heard that in the Kingdom of Grace, people who had done nothing to earn it would get to be people they had no right to be and that they would get to do things that they had done nothing to deserve. Within a few minutes, this centurion, this symbol of oppression and military might and privilege and idolatry, suddenly not only got his servant healed, but became a model of great faith, whom, Jesus said, all people would learn from in the future.

Then Jesus met the woman at the well.[27] Another non-Jew, another sexually confused outcast, another person whose life was a broken mess. Someone who would have ticked all the boxes in an "ineligibility for the Kingdom" application. As a non-Jew living in Samaria she would have understood some things. She would have understood something about religious practice and proper procedure for worship. She would have known who you have to be, and what you had to do to get on in life. And she would have known that she was on the outside.

She said that Jews shouldn't associate themselves with Samaritans.

Jesus said it was going to be different from now on.

She said that her fathers worshipped on the mountain and the Jews worshipped in Jerusalem.

Jesus said it was going to be different from now on.

Jesus told her that from now on, people were not going to be excluded from joining the party because of their ethnic origin, background, or social status. Who people were, and where people came from was not going to be the determining factor any more. From now on people were not going to get to worship because of who they were. They were going to get to worship because of who He was. He announced to this wayward woman that the Kingdom of Grace was for her, and He announced the

---

26 Matthew 8:8.
27 John 4:1–26.

new basis for worship that she could be part of. He said that in the Kingdom of Grace, people who had done nothing to earn it would get to be people they had no right to be, and they would get to do things that they had done nothing to deserve. People would get to be part of the Kingdom of God, and to worship in the presence of God, not because of who they were, but because of who He was.

There was to be no more inside and no more outside. There was just a level playing field.

The mountains were being laid low – through grace.

The valleys were being raised up – through grace.

The rough ground was being levelled – through grace.

And all of mankind could be part of it together.[28]

The first were becoming last and the last were becoming first.[29] This was not a new hierarchy being introduced. It was a removal of hierarchy. Jesus was flinging wide the doors of the Kingdom to everyone and anyone who wanted it.

When Jesus went into the temple grounds and turned over all the traders' tables,[30] He was not only condemning people for allowing the making of money out of worship to overshadow the enactment of worship itself, but He was making a further announcement of grace.[31] The outer courts of the temple were as far as Gentiles could go in the old hierarchy, but even this place had been effectively dismantled as a place where they could come and worship. By His actions Jesus was not only reaffirming the past covenant with Abraham, but He was announcing the new age of grace where these old concepts of inside and outside would be blown wide apart – so wide that

---

28 Isaiah 40:4–5.

29 Matthew 20:16.

30 Matthew 21:12.

31 There was clearly good sense in traders being in the outer courts of the temple. People would come from far afield to worship there, and it was far easier for them to bring money with them so they could purchase sacrificial animals than to bring the animals with them. However, it seems that the commercial aspects of this trade had become the focus, even making the outer courts inaccessible to the Gentiles for worship.

they cease to exist. Forever.

Can you see how irrational this Kingdom of Grace was?

It was so irrational that a thief on a cross, presumably there as a result of a lifetime of sin, gets to make a last-gasp confession that means he inherits all the fullness of heaven – peace, joy, and life everlasting.[32] It was so irrational that the workers who turn up and work for the last hour of the day got to be paid as much as someone who had been slaving away since sunrise.[33]

Hardly fair, in my book.

But grace isn't fair.

When Jesus died on the cross, next to that repentant thief, He sealed the deal. Grace was made available for whosoever believed in Him.[34] The unmerited, undeserved, unabating, unrationed, unrelenting, irrational favour of God was something that would never have to be earned ever again.

It was something that would just be received.

Not earned.

Not purchased through superior intellect.

Not gained through political manoeuvring.

Not inherited from your parents.

Not won as a result of physical prowess.

Not qualified for at some theological college.

Just received.

Later, Saul, this evil-murderer-soon-to-become-world-famous-leader who was there when Stephen was martyred for his faith, approving of what was going on,[35] was found out by grace too.[36] As the renamed Paul said in a letter to Timothy:

> Even though I was once a blasphemer and a persecutor
> and a violent man, I was shown mercy because I acted
> in ignorance and unbelief. The grace of our Lord was

---

32 Luke 23:43.
33 Matthew 20:1–16.
34 John 3:16.
35 Acts 7:54–60.
36 Acts 9:1–19.

poured out on me abundantly, along with the faith and love that are in Christ Jesus.[37]

Paul himself, who had done nothing to earn it, got to be someone he had no right to be, and got to do things that he had done nothing to deserve. Despite his background and upbringing and social status, Paul got to be one of the most significant church leaders, most widely travelled evangelists, most prolific Bible writers ever.

No wonder, then, that Paul, who knew so much grace, walked his life in grace.

Paul names grace as the reason he carried on through suffering.[38] He talks of God's grace that builds people up.[39] He said that he thought himself only qualified to preach because of grace.[40] He said that spiritual gifts were gifts of grace.[41] He acknowledged his calling as coming from grace.[42] He said that anything built of worth was built through grace.[43] He desired to conduct himself not through worldly wisdom but with grace.[44] He talked of the incomparable riches of God's grace.[45] He urged people to be strong in grace.[46] He said that in times of need we would know grace, and that grace was sufficient.[47] He even said that our conversations should always be full of grace.[48] In fact almost every letter Paul wrote in the New Testament begins and ends with grace.

Paul perpetuated the new way of the Kingdom that Jesus embodied, and taught, and lived in, and died for: that you didn't have to earn grace, you just had to receive it. As Paul puts it in

---

37 1 Timothy 1:13–14.
38 Acts 20:24.
39 Acts 20:32.
40 Ephesians 3:8.
41 Romans 12:6.
42 Galatians 1:15.
43 1 Corinthians 3:10.
44 2 Corinthians 1:12.
45 Ephesians 2:7.
46 2 Timothy 2:1.
47 2 Corinthians 12:9.
48 Colossians 4:6.

Romans 11: "And if by grace, then it is no longer by works; if it were, grace would no longer be grace."[49]

This grace was unconditional.

In fact, as soon as we put conditions on grace, it stops being grace.

We can see how Paul was totally convinced about this when you read about his confrontation with the leaders of the wider church in Judea in Acts 15. When it was suggested that grace was somehow limited, or purchased through works, we read how he came into "sharp disagreement" with such views. Now I'm not sure what this "sharp disagreement" looked like. It sounds a bit polite and English to me. But I suspect that, as Paul was from a country more known for passion than diplomacy, it was not a gentle conversation. Such was Paul's experience of grace, and his godly wisdom about grace, and his total conviction that you can't build the Kingdom without it, that he became such a great advocate of it.

Yes, the story of the Bible is the story of grace, a story that culminates in Revelation where we see grace's crowning glory: the Lamb on the throne – and the river of grace pouring from the throne.

And the final words of the whole Bible?

"Grace... be with God's people."[50]

Not money, not power, not wealth, not political status, not righteousness, not glory, not faith, not wisdom, not health, but grace.

Grace be with God's people.

I don't find it at all strange that the final words in the Scriptures are about grace.

You see, on the final day, as we stand with Christ and are found in Him, we will stand only because of grace.

And as His people move from this age to the next, we will live on because of grace.

---

49 Romans 11:6.
50 Revelation 22:21.

The invitation of grace: God's invitation to worship

When we gather on a Sunday to sing, we gather as a people who have done nothing to earn it, we get to be people we have no right to be, and we get to do something that we don't deserve. Despite our shame and our rebellion and our disobedience, we get to be called sons of God. We get to stand before Him, to worship Him, to experience His holy presence and receive His blessings.

In the past people had to go through a whole range of processes and procedures to get close, and even if you did all of that stuff, only one person – the person more on the inside than anyone else – got to go into the most holy place.

Just once a year, just one person got to go into the most holy place.

But in the Kingdom of Grace, things are different.

We all get to be on the very inside.

We all get to be in the most holy place.

And in that moment we find ourselves on a level playing field where no one is better qualified to be there than anyone else, where no one is more deserving than his or her neighbour. We are all there because the Kingdom of Grace is so wide, so irrational, so undeserved that it embraces even us.

So when we join before the throne of God and sing, our status, upbringing, ministry effort, or background all become as nothing. We gather together before the throne of grace, and we are just happy to be there. The national speaker, the check-out assistant, the drug addict, the sexually confused, the unemployed, the millionaire, the high-flyer, the oppressed, and the abused. We gather together and stand in the river. Allowing it to wash over us, cleanse us, satisfy us, heal us.

We all gather together before the throne of grace, and we are just happy to be there.

Blessed.

A seat called mercy: The crowning glory of God's character

The ark was the most potent symbol of God's presence. His greatness, His splendour, His majesty, His glory, His holiness. The ark of the covenant contained the tablets of stone on which were carved the laws of God. They were given to Moses at Mount Sinai, and they represented the holy ways of God, representing His rule and reign and majesty and kingship.

The ark was important.

And holy.

This ark was opened once, and some people looked inside when they knew they shouldn't. They were struck down. The ark was once carried amongst the people of God in a way that was not prescribed. Someone died. The ark was once put in a temple built for other gods, and stood overnight amongst the graven images of those gods. Those other gods fell down and broke into pieces.

Clearly, the ark was not something that was to be messed with.

God's holiness is not something that is to be messed with. Because when people mess with it, they have a habit of dying.

Then once its travels were complete, the ark resided in the inner place in the Temple in Jerusalem. It resided in the most holy place within the most holy building within the most holy city. It resided in the holiest of all holy places. Only once a year was someone allowed into this most holy place. Such was the amazing otherness of God and the ark that symbolized His most otherly presence.

His get-too-close-and-you-will-probably-die otherness.

His get-this-wrong-and-you-may-fall-as-dust holiness.

But on the top of the ark, on top of this incredible symbol of God's greatness, splendour, majesty, glory, reign and holiness was a seat.

A seat called mercy.

Made of gold, and crowned on the top of the ark was a symbol of God's unmerited favour.

Gold, this most precious of all created materials, was placed on the top of the ark, the most potent symbol of God's holiness, to illustrate the most amazing characteristic of God's character.

Mercy.

God has always been, and will always be, a God of mercy, a God who wants to draw people back to Himself, who continually courts the affection of His world.

His mercy sits as the crowning glory on His holiness.

From the day the ark came into existence shortly after one man called Moses stood on the top of a mountain, the message of mercy was carved in gold for all to see. Then many years later another Man stood on top of a mountain and reaffirmed God's heart of mercy, His heart of mercy that can reach even me, even you. His mercy that can reach everyone through His grace. And three years later this same Man stood in our place and took the punishment that we deserved and in doing so, fulfilled everything that God requires to make a very, very easy pathway for us to be close to Him.

All those requirements for the burnt offerings?[51]

Covered.

All those requirements for sin offerings?[52]

Sorted.

All that stuff that we had to go through to establish and sustain closeness to God?

Done.

Through Jesus.

By grace.

Forever.

And one day, when heaven-space and earth-space become one, and we return to the perfect state we were always intended

---

51 Leviticus 1.
52 Leviticus 4.

for, we will dwell there because of grace – the unmerited, undeserved, unabating, unrationed, unrelenting, irrational favour of God.

The ultimate expression of grace: The cross of Jesus

On 8 November 1987 eleven people were killed when a bomb planted by the IRA exploded in Enniskillen, Northern Ireland, during a Remembrance Day ceremony at the town's cenotaph. Ten of the dead were civilians. One of the dead was Marie Wilson, the daughter of Gordon Wilson.

Gordon Wilson recounted how his daughter lay dying beneath the rubble as he held her hand through the debris. Later, in an interview with the BBC, Wilson described with anguish his last conversation with his daughter and his feelings towards her killers: "She held my hand tightly, and gripped me as hard as she could. She said, 'Daddy, I love you very much.' Those were her exact words to me, and those were the last words I ever heard her say."

Then to the astonishment of listeners, Wilson went on to add, "But I bear no ill will. I bear no grudge. Dirty sort of talk is not going to bring her back to life. She was a great wee lassie. She loved her profession. She was a pet. She's dead. She's in heaven and we shall meet again. I will pray for these men tonight and every night."

As the historian Jonathan Bardon recounts: "No words in more than twenty-five years of violence in Northern Ireland had such a powerful, emotional impact."[53] In fact many people think that the events surrounding 8 November 1987 were the beginning of the end of violence in the region. Whether this act of forgiveness – this act of grace – from Gordon Wilson towards his daughter's killers was a big part of that, I don't think anyone can tell. My own opinion is that it was. And certainly it was clear

53 Taken from William Ury's book *The Third Side*, Penguin, 1999.

that Gordon Wilson believed that an act of grace was the only way that peace was going to come to Northern Ireland.

The journey that this loving father's daughter took ended up in an extremely awful place, buried beneath the rubble caused by some very awful people, and she was later to die on the operating table. The act of grace offered from this father, was to forgive those who caused him so much heartache.

I started this chapter by saying how grace comes naturally to me with my daughters, and how I felt that whatever journey they went on, that grace would always triumph, that grace would always win the day. But of course, I never imagine that the grace I would have to extend would be not to them, but to their murderers, their killers. I can't imagine how much that would cost me, or hurt me, or anger me. Yet to a world that beat up, spat on, and murdered His Son, God still shows grace, still courts its affection.

I don't know where you are with God at the moment. I don't know whether you are in a good place or a bad place, whether you are walking closely with Him, or have totally messed up in life. But wherever you are, isn't it a mind-numbing thought that God is still courting you?

This is probably a dreadful confession from a worship pastor, but sometimes the events surrounding the cross, the suffering Jesus underwent, and the pain the Father endured seems remote, part of history, part of a story that I read and understand and am thankful for, but never really feel. So often when I gather amongst my friends and sing songs to God in church, the cross seems distant. I wonder whether this is the case because, in the busyness of life and ministry, in my attempts to be relevant and skilful and productive and fruitful and culturally aware, when I come to worship I lose sight of something so incredible.

I don't really deserve to be here, to do this, but by the grace of God shown through the cross, I am, and I can.

Cross-centred worship: Keeping grace at the heart of worship

If worship is at the heart of our relationship with God, and if grace is the foundation for that worship, and the cross is the means by which we know that grace, then we need to understand that worship will be messy, full of contradictions. It will involve people we don't like, even people who we don't think should be around us, let alone inside our church building opening their mouths and joining in with our songs.

We read with amazement the story of an oppressive power-hungry centurion and we learn more about grace – but what if it was one of our children who had been enslaved and abused by this person? How would we feel then if Jesus affirmed him as a man of faith?

We rejoice in the story of a prostitute being told her worship was beautiful and historic – but what if this woman had slept with our husband, broken up our marriage, and destroyed our children's security? How much rejoicing would we do then?

We celebrate the way Jesus deals with a corrupt tax collector and gives him dignity, but what if this tax collector had stolen our money, defrauded our family, caused us to lose our home and livelihood? How much celebrating would we be doing then? How would we feel about the fact that Jesus went to this tax collector's home for a meal – possibly even the home that he had bought with money stolen from us?

We love the way Jesus revealed himself to an evil murderer, turned his life around, and gave him an amazing ministry. But what if this man had killed our son, our daughter, our mother or father? How would we feel about him leading our church then?

How would we feel about standing beside these people in church and singing songs to God?

There is nothing particularly aesthetically pleasing about the cross: a rough wooden instrument of torture, standing on a rubbish heap, dripping with blood, engulfed by the smell of excrement, surrounded by broken, confused, morally bankrupt people shouting their abuse; but if grace is the foundation of our worship, then we have to be people of that cross, however much we find that its implications shock us.

So, let's not undermine the centrality of the cross in our worship. Let's not reduce the suffering of Jesus to a side-story in our churches, our liturgies, and our songs. Let's not be shy, or embarrassed by its symbolism and reality for us.

When the cross becomes central to our worship, we find that our eyes are lifted off ourselves and our circumstances and set upon Jesus. We find that we are singing more about Him than about us. We find that the emphasis on "I" that so often dominates worship these days is replaced by an emphasis on "You". We will be people who come to the throne of God in worship not as consumers who are looking for a thrill, but as blessed sinners, happy to be close to God.

When the cross becomes central to our worship, any sense of stardom, ego, achievement, or status becomes crucified, and we find that those of us in leadership of worship are just as poor in spirit as those we lead the worship for, but together we become rich in Christ crucified. Through grace.

When the cross becomes central to our worship, we find that we become people of justice, intent on expressing the welcome and belonging we find on the holy ground before God – something that not only drives us to the broken of the world around us, but longs to gather them and welcome them into our midst. We will be people who see the unjust events that took Jesus to His death burn within us and compel us to confront the injustice in our world. Through grace.

When the cross becomes central to our worship, we find that a celebration of the Last Supper becomes full of meaning. It becomes something that is seen as an essential and powerful part of our welcome to those who need Christ, rather than seen as a barrier to their journey towards God. We find that the very mystery that surrounds the bread and the wine becomes a wonder that draws people to Jesus. Through grace.

When the cross becomes central to our worship we become people who are compelled to live lives of whole-hearted radical discipleship. The willingness of Jesus to surrender all in an act of worship to the Father causes us to respond ourselves in glad surrender, running the race of this life to the very end.

And when the cross becomes central to our worship we find that our hearts are set upon the hope we have in Christ, that the Lamb who became nothing for us, was crucified for us, humbled for us, wounded for us, is the same Lamb that will one day be seen by all people – crowned in glory, ruling in justice, and reigning in power.

> *Speak to this heart of the love that is my treasure:*
> *Love so unbounded, so faithful and so true.*
> *Strength in my weakness, my comfort and my shelter,*
> *That stills my hunger and sets my soul at rest.*
>
> *Speak to this heart of the cross that shows your mercy.*
> *Steadfast in purpose, the Christ was crucified*
> *Humbled and wounded, all majesty surrendered.*
> *The Father's favour revealed in suffering*
>
> *Speak to this heart of the truth that is Your gospel*
> *Death is defeated and sinners justified*
> *My sure foundation, the rock of our salvation*
> *Jesus the Saviour has set this captive free.*
>
> *Speak to this heart of the hope that is made certain:*
> *Love's crowning glory, the Lamb upon the throne,*
> *Risen exalted. In this my heart rejoices.*
> *I live in Him and forever He shall reign.*[54]

---

54 "Speak to this heart", Neil Bennetts, © 2005 Trinity Publishing.

Chapter 3

The Scent of a Woman

PERSONAL DEVOTION IN WORSHIP

Simon Ponsonby

This story is about personal devotion in worship.

Worship that is extravagant and expressive, the spirit of which is an example for us all. We see a woman worshipping in an unfettered, unbridled, and unreserved way. It is told in all four Gospels. Each apostle was impacted by it, each contributing distinct details which impressed themselves on the author.

Feet, tears, hair, love, faith, forgiveness, fragrant.

Luke locates it at the home of a Pharisee[55] where the woman kisses Jesus' feet, and washes them with tears, and dries them with her hair. The attention is on the feet of Christ here, the same feet that soon will be covered in blood and twisted in agony, pinned by rough iron to rough wood. I wonder if Luke was thinking this was an enactment of the psalmist's exhortation: "Exalt the Lord our God; worship at his footstool!"[56]

In Luke's account the Pharisee is offended by this woman and questions whether Jesus is truly a prophet, since he appears not to know what kind of a woman this is – an unclean woman, a prostitute. The Pharisee expected Jesus to rebuke this unclean woman. Instead Jesus rebukes the Pharisee for not showing him the customary greeting of a kiss, nor honouring his guest by anointing his head with oil. The Pharisee is a picture of worship

55 Luke 7:36–50.
56 Psalm 99:5.

withheld, not kissing Christ, not blessing Christ. The prostitute is a picture of unrestrained worship. Jesus tells a parable to explain why she worshipped thus and concludes: "her many sins have been forgiven – as her great love has shown. But whoever has been forgiven little loves little". He then tells the woman, "Your faith has saved you; go in peace."

True worship is the expression of love, of faith. Loving Christ and faith in the saving Christ are evidenced by true worship – intimate, passionate, abandoned self-offering to Jesus. It is not the worship that saves, but it is the worship that shows the saving faith.

John (12:1) places the event six days before the Passover – a Saturday night – when the customary Jewish way to end solemn Passover was by dining with friends. The meal in Bethany was thrown in honour of Lazarus who had been raised from dead, and the woman is revealed as none other than Lazarus' sister – Mary, the one who buried herself at Jesus' feet while Martha busied herself.

John offers a beautiful touch: "the house was filled with the fragrance of the perfume".[57] Surely that is a picture of what worship should produce, the very atmosphere scented with the fragrance of adoration. Worship should overflow. More than a two-way, "I–Thou" encounter and response of beloved to lover, of created to Creator, the chemistry of true worship produces an overflow that is perceived by others, filling the room.

For the remainder of this chapter we will turn our attention to Mark's magnificent account in his chapter 14. (But in doing so, let us not forget the accents that the other Gospels show – worship that is withheld by the religious, and offered by the prostitute; worship that is tactile, emotional, sensual, even – hair, tears, feet, scent, kisses – total self-offering motivated by sentiments of love and faith, forgiveness and salvation.)

In Mark 14, as wicked men plot, worship is poured out.

---

57 John 12:3.

The carrion crows crowd in to take a piece of Christ.[58] Jesus is seeking comfort with his friends at a meal in Bethany (verse 3). Simon the leper is offering hospitality. Obviously he is a healed leper and not in social isolation, as his condition would have warranted. I wonder if Jesus had healed him, and then characteristically invited Himself to dinner!

In fact we know that Jesus was interested in the whole of human life, never just the eternal destiny of souls. He called Zacchaeus down from the tree and went and ate with his friends. He went with Matthew the tax-collector to a party at his house. And now here is Jesus eating with a leper he's healed! Jesus was a dinner-party goer. He enjoyed shared food, shared company. Not just religious meetings and sermons and theology, but everyday life lived together. Shared humanity.

Without waiting to be welcomed, a woman obtrusively gatecrashes the meal. She seems utterly unself-conscious, oblivious to the others in the room. It's as if there is no one else in the room. Indeed, for her there really isn't!

This woman is gloriously preoccupied with worshipping Jesus.

C. S. Lewis once wrote: "The perfect church service would be one we were... unaware of – our attention would have [just] been on God." In the words of the famous hymn, this woman knew what it meant to be "lost in wonder, love and praise".[59]

Her worship was valuable

A woman came with an alabaster flask of ointment of pure nard, very costly.[60]

Nard was a rare spice extracted from the spikenard root that was native to India. Its beauty, rarity, and the lengthy, hazardous journey along the trade routes to Israel meant its price was

---

58 Mark 14:1.
59 C. S. Lewis, *Letters to Malcolm: Chiefly on Prayer*, Harvest Press, 1964, pp. 4–5.
60 Mark 14:3.

exceptional. The first-century Roman historian Pliny tells us that it "holds the foremost possible rank amongst perfumes". The NIV speaks of it being "worth a year's wage" (14:5). Another interpretation of the original Greek text states its worth at 300 denarii, where 1 denarius was a typical day's pay for a labourer.

This phial of oil was worth, in today's terms, perhaps £15,000. This rare and valuable gift, a year's wages, was what she was going to worship with.

I have some dear friends who, in 1998, moved by this very story of the gift of "a year's wages", actually remortgaged their house, adding the equivalent of a full year's salary onto the mortgage, and gave the lot in a gift of abandoned worship to God. And God has certainly honoured them for it.

The value of this gift given in worship is further compounded by the structure and description in the Greek text which attaches four adjectival genitives to *alabastron* (the alabaster phial): "of perfume", "of nard", "of pure", "of costly". Each one of these "adjectives" intensifies the sense of how special this gift was.

We don't know where this single woman acquired such a valuable thing. In the days before banks, people often kept their wealth in goods like this, or in jewellery. Some commentators note that life savings were not kept in banks but in tangible assets such as nard. It is quite plausible, if we triangulate Mark's account with Luke's (7:39 – "If this man were a prophet, he would have known who and what sort of woman this is who is touching him, for she is a sinner [prostitute]"), that this perfume was the fruit of her earnings, or even a gift from a high-class Roman officer lover. Perhaps it was even a tool of her trade – the sort of accessory used by a very high-class prostitute to cover the stench of sin!

But to Jesus, and for us, the issue was not where she got it but where she gave it.

This was an item of royal worth, a truly kingly gift.

She gave it to her King!

What she gave showed the worth she gave to Christ.

How much do you think Jesus is worth? Our worship will never rise higher than our vision and value of Jesus. If we truly see Him as our Lord, and Saviour, and King, both Lover and God – then nothing is too good for Him. He will get all we have. Worship given is an indicator of the worth we hold someone in.

There is a parallel to be seen in 1 Chronicles 21. David wishes to sacrifice an offering to God and build an altar on the site of Araunah's threshing floor where God's judgment against Israel ceased. Araunah, the owner, offers David the site for free, but David adamantly refuses (verse 24): "No, but I will buy them for the full price. I will not take for the Lord what is yours, nor offer burnt offerings that cost me nothing"! Worship that costs us nothing is worth what it costs – nothing! Worship that costs us something is worth what it costs – something.

Song-writer and worship leader Dave Fellingham once said: "True worship needs to be demonstrated." This woman actually says nothing, but her actions speak louder than words! Her gift says it all. Some of us are happy to sing to Jesus until the cows come home – but we must recognize that lip-service at a church service is not worship!

Her worship was total

> She broke the flask and poured it [the perfume] over
> his head.[61]

This action of breaking shows her intention of giving Jesus everything. There was no holding back, no going back, no taking back, no putting back the nard into the vase. It is spent, in full. This woman doesn't just dribble a drop and save the rest for a rainy day. Jesus gets it all. As the hymn says, "All to Jesus, all to Jesus, all to thee I freely give."

---

61 Mark 14:3.

True worship is never measured out – it is a sacrifice of praise.

In the Old Testament, various sacrifices were given in worship – they were "burnt offerings", not sin offerings, but free acts of worship in which the offering was totally burnt. No part was kept by the priests to be consumed. The burnt offering symbolized that everything was given irrevocably as a sweet aroma, pleasing to God.[62]

Worship burns bridges to any and all other claims to rule our hearts.

True worship says that God is valued above all other worldly worth.

True worship says "take it all".

In Luke and John's telling of this event, they add that besides anointing with oil, this woman let down her hair and wiped Jesus' feet with it.

We cannot comprehend how culturally incredible such an act was. Feet trampled in dusty, sewage-strewn streets were an appendage of disgrace, unclean. Yet it's Jesus' lesser, ignoble feature that is the object of her great honouring. In stark contrast to the "ignoble feet", a woman's hair was her honour, her glory. Women covered their heads, and never showed their hair except to their husband! A Jewish woman always kept her hair veiled. The only man ever to see it unfurled was her husband. Indeed, in some branches of strict modern Judaism, wives will shave their heads after their husbands have seen this glory, and will ever thereafter wear a wig, their beauty shown and known by only one man.

Revealed hair was a symbol of profound intimacy, and this woman gives what she has, what she can to Jesus. All her glory is for his glory. This woman comes and uncovers her hair, unfurls it and then wipes her tears off Jesus' feet. This is a deeply vulnerable, even sensual act. "I give you everything!" I am reminded of the wedding vows: "All my worldly goods I thee endow – with my

---

62 Leviticus 1:9.

body I thee honour."

I watched a TV programme following several couples trekking across the desert. Before they started, the SAS guide went through their kit to remove all unnecessary items that added extra weight. One travels light in the wilderness.

One woman refused to leave her make-up bag behind.

Even in the desert, for a woman, it is important to look good!

I love that image in Exodus 38:8 when the women of Israel tramping through the desert come to Moses and give him, for God, an offering of their mirrors for making the laver, the washing-basin for the priests' services in the tabernacle. It is as if they were saying: "We care more about how God's tabernacle looks than how we look!"

That is worship. Costly, self-giving worship. That's what this woman is doing – she doesn't care about herself, she doesn't care what she looks like, what others think of her. All she wants to do is to honour, adore, pour herself out on Jesus.

In verse 8 Mark tells us Jesus said: "She has done what she could." Indeed, she did all she could! This woman could not do better if she tried. She gave her best.

Nearly every school report I ever had said "Could do better"! I wonder – if the Lord wrote a worship report on me, would He say the same?

Frances Havergall was a worshipper. A total worshipper. Inspired by this passage, she wrote the famous hymn about giving Christ all: "Take my love, my Lord, I pour, at thy feet, its treasure store." In 1878, four years after writing that hymn, Miss Havergall wrote to a friend:

The Lord has shown me another little step, and, of course, I have taken it with extreme delight, shipping off all my ornaments to the Church Missionary House, including a jewel cabinet that is really fit for a countess, where all will be accepted and disposed of for me.

Nearly fifty articles are being packed up. I don't think I
ever packed a box with such pleasure.

True worship was not just beautiful words but beautiful deeds,
total giving to God.

We can worship and should worship not merely with words
sung, or declarations made, but with fragrant offerings and
sacrifices, with costly love-gifts given. We can give our time to
God's service as worship, we can give our money to God's people
and cause as worship, we can give our affections to God as
worship, we can give our gifts and talents to God as worship.

Worship is a gift given.

Her worship was a battle

There were some who said to themselves indignantly,
"Why was the ointment wasted like that?" ... And they
scolded her.[63]

The Greek word Mark uses to describe the emotion of their
response is *enebrimonto*. It is used to describe a snorting horse.
Those present were indignant, angry, offended, insulted and
reacted aggressively.

"What a waste this worship is!" they sneered. "An immoral,
absurd extravagance!"

"Disgusting."

"Wrong at every level."

Surely, their accusation of waste shows how little they
understood worship. Their accusation of waste shows how little
they understood Jesus – what He is worth, what worship He
welcomes. Surely it was they who, despite three years with Jesus,
had wasted so much time, while failing to recognize Jesus and
give Him his due. Their indignant, harsh scolding of the woman
is a reaction out of all proportion.

---

63 Mark 14:4–5.

It is bizarre.

It is demonic.

It comes in the guise of concern for the poor, but I suspect they are not so concerned for the poor, as they are contemptuous for the woman and her worship.

Sometimes, a rebuke can come to our worship in the subtle guise of spirituality. We can be made to feel as if our worship is "unspiritual" – told that our worship and praise is not honouring God because it's too loud, too long, too simple, not aesthetically beautiful, self-indulgent. This woman was accused of being wasteful; the accusers were making out that they were being compassionate towards the poor.

When I was a toddler, my mum was given a large jar of most expensive Chanel No. 5 oil by my uncle. In those rather austere days, this was an extravagant gift, something my mother would never ever have treated herself to. One day, something possessed me to go into the bathroom, get the bottle from the shelf, unscrew the cap, and empty the lot down the bath plug-hole! The bathroom smelt wonderful for days. My ears probably smarted for days. My mum was indignant; she had every right to be. What I did with mum's perfume was waste. But what this worshipper did with her perfume was no waste, it was pure worship.

Watchman Nee in his book *The Normal Christian Life*, reflecting on this rebuke of wasteful worship, wrote: "Oh to be wasted – it is a blessed thing to be wasted for the Lord – many of us have been used but we do not know what it means to be wasted."

The twentieth-century Swiss theologian Karl Barth, commenting on the disciples' sharp rebuke of this woman, wrote: "Paganism flourishes vehemently in the vacuum left by this true worship." On first hearing, this comment seems too sharp. These were the Twelve. They followed Christ. Surely they were not pagan! Yet they balk at the true worship given to Christ and they themselves have never entered into nor expressed true worship.

Paganism is false worship or withheld worship – the pagan protests against true worship. And the disciples, and the host, are in danger of paganism.

Worship, in spirit and truth, will always be a sign spoken against!

Her heart was for worship. A. W. Tozer wrote: "I would rather worship God than do anything." So would this woman, regardless of the regard of others. Sadly, the devil wants her and us to do anything other than worship God. The devil will always mock and militate against worship, laying accusations against extravagant, heart-felt, abandoned worship as worthless waste. The devil will always want to redirect our money, mouth, and heart from the honour of Jesus – even disguising it as something good, even work for the poor.

When Abel offered a "better" sacrifice to God, darkness caused Cain to slay the worshipper.

When, through Moses, God asked Pharaoh, "Let my people go that they might worship me", Pharaoh increased their burden and forbade their worship.

When David stripped and danced before ark, Michal despised him and was rebuked.

We noted earlier, and it's worth revisiting, how at Jesus' birth, when the Wise Men came "to worship the one born king of the Jews", Herod, with demonic jealousy, commanded all baby boys to be killed so that this one baby, the incarnate Son of God, would not be worshipped.

Following Jesus' baptism, when He was led by the Spirit into the wilderness, the devil tempted Him away from His vocation, the central issue being worship: "all this I will give you if you worship me". Jesus replied, "Worship God and serve him only". I believe He was referring to Himself at this point, as if saying, "I won't worship and serve you – you will worship and serve me!"

Then at Jesus' triumphal entry, as the children cried

"Hosanna", the Pharisees sought to silence it. But Jesus said, "If you stop them, the stones will cry out."

There is a war on worship because the enemy of our souls knows our worship is warfare. Do not be surprised if, when you set your heart to worship, war starts. As you praise, your mind may often be bombarded by dark thoughts, or simply distractions from devotion. We must persevere, pressing through the enemy's indignation to that place of delighting the Lord. Mary may have heard the protests of the others about her worship; she may have seen the look of disgust on their faces, the sneering or mocking or condemning of her devotion. But all that mattered was Christ, her Christ, and the protestations of men would not prevent her from worship.

Her worship was beautiful

But Jesus said, "Leave her alone. Why do you trouble her? She has done a beautiful thing to me."[64]

Mother Teresa poured out her life for the poor in the slums of Calcutta. When asked why she did it by Malcolm Muggeridge, a rather cynical communist satirist, she replied: "I wanted to do something beautiful for God." So beautiful was this gracious gift that it moved Muggeridge towards becoming a Christian! Mary's actions enraged some, embarrassed others, but enchanted Jesus. What others thought was "dreadful" Jesus described as "beautiful". Those who were indignant dismissed her (in Luke's account) for being "that kind of woman" – impure, unclean. But Jesus described her worship as *kalos* – translated generally as "beautiful". It also contained a moral quality, something pure and perfect.

Pure worship somehow reconstitutes the impure as pure.

"Beautiful worship" need not be technically and aesthetically

---

64 Mark 14:6.

perfect. Indeed, it can be out of tune, out of key, out of time, but still beautiful to God.

I enjoy the work of the sixteenth-century English composer Thomas Tallis. His most famous work is *Spem in Alium*, a remarkable forty-part choral piece. The sculptor and artist Janet Cardiff, using a forty-track recorder, taped each individual part of *Spem*, sung by Salisbury Cathedral choir. Then in a round gallery, she set up forty speakers, each playing a single voice. You could put your ear to a speaker and hear each chorister, or stand in the middle and hear all the choir.

It was technologically, aesthetically, and musically incredible. By any standard, beautiful, but not necessarily worshipful. Worship may be utterly absent in the heart and mind of the listener and the choir.

But Jesus says that a former prostitute pouring out oil on His head and kissing His feet, wetting them with tears, wiping them with her hair, is a "beautiful thing". Even as the nard was "pure", so her offering was pure – undiluted, unadulterated, unmixed worship.

Jesus says this woman has done something "to me". The Greek words are *en emoi*, literally meaning "in and to me", and this further underscores how deeply Jesus felt the event. Jesus spent His whole life pouring out His life for others. Few bothered to come and even say thank you. Many were hostile or aggressive, but here, at last, was someone who asked for nothing but gave her everything. I expect the angels, so often amazed at the paucity of praise given to Christ the King, held their breath in awe and then turned to one another, pointing at this woman, saying, "At last, someone gets it!" – and then let out a huge, great cheer!

This wasn't for her benefit, or the benefit of the poor. Jesus wasn't given worship out of a sense of duty, nor was He extracting it indirectly, by proxy, as when a deed is done for the poor.

Jesus was receiving direct, exclusive, undiluted devotion; this was just for Jesus.

When my boys were very young I would often try to take them out for treats – in particular they loved ice-cream parlours. I would order a giant knickerbocker glory: several scoops of flavoured ice-cream, chopped banana, strawberries, nuts, drizzled with maple syrup, then covered with chocolates and Jelly Babies. On one occasion, on being presented with this giant dessert, I recall Joel asking, eyes popping out and mouth wide open, "Is that mine? All of it? A whole one?"

This was the only incident in Christ's whole life and ministry where someone gave something just for Him! She gave all of it, just for Jesus.

Some years ago I stayed with dear friends in Manchester. They knew I had the palate, if not the pay, for fine wine. They took out a bottle of fifty-year-old port given them at their wedding twenty-five years earlier. And they opened it for me. I protested that this was a remarkable gift given to them and should be enjoyed just by them on their next wedding anniversary. But my friend Robin resisted: "Simon, there is no one we'd rather drink it with." To them it was sentimental, valuable, and sacrificial. To me it was an extravagant gift of love and friendship. Some may have considered it wasteful. To me it was beautiful.

What this woman did for Jesus was beautiful!

Her worship was a symbol

She has anointed my body beforehand for burial.[65]

Her worship was also a prophetic symbol – it was worship which witnessed. She said nothing but what she did spoke volumes. Her worship somehow echoes Jesus' own story. It is prophetic in that it points beyond itself to something God would reveal. Her worship tells us not only about her devotion to Christ, but also hints at a revelation of Christ. It is not just about her love, but her Lord.

---

65 Mark 14:8.

This beautiful thing she did for Jesus mirrors the beautiful thing Jesus does for us: the broken beautiful vase mirrors Christ's broken beautiful body; the poured out priceless liquid mirrors the blood of Christ poured out for us.

Oil was used to anoint kings and priests.[66] Oil was poured over Jesus, who is the King of Kings and our great High Priest. Oil was poured over items used in facilitating worship in the tabernacle.[67] Jesus is the focus of worship and encountering God. Oil was poured over the dead, to cover the stench of decomposition. The oil speaks of anointing Christ, who was shortly to die.

Her worship is a symbol of her costly devotion to Christ, while at the same time a prophetic symbol of her revelation of the crucified Christ.

Worship is not about us, it's about God. Not for our benefit, but God's.

Worship is to God, and yet it may also speak about God to others who see us worship. Worship is prophetic, communicative. I'm not talking about the crafted, scripted, so-called "sacred dance" sort of worship where movements are choreographed drama and rather obvious – I'm talking about worship from the heart, through the humanity of the individual, which someone speaks to, but also about, God.

In the worship in heaven, as depicted in Revelation 6, we see worship which witnesses. We see day and night, singing, honouring, and thanksgiving directed to the Lamb on the throne. We read of the worshippers falling down before the Lamb, laying their crowns at his feet! This is in the present tense, and we are not to think of this as a one-off, once-only liturgical act. It is a repeated drama – the saints are crowned and they lay these crowns at the feet of the Lamb. And maybe – who knows? – the angels hand them back to the recipients, who say, no, not for us, not unto us, but to the Lamb who sits on the throne. The

---

66 2 Kings 9.
67 Exodus 30.

prostrating in obeisance and reverence, the casting of crowns of honour and glory before the Lamb, symbolize that it is Jesus who is the focus, the point, the purpose of worship.

Worship flows one way – it is all to Him, it is all for Him.

If someone was watching you in worship, what would they deduce about your relationship with the Lord and the Lord you worship? I grew up in a strict chapel context where it seemed that old people, in cold places, sang old hymns, on crumbling pianos with words that were archaic – hands in pockets, no movement, no enjoyment, little effort. I am sure some worshipped from the heart – but what did that teach a young boy about God? It suggested that God was old, cold, plain, rather lifeless, rather serious; little texture, little colour, little vigour.

What does someone infer about God when they enter a church and see a little red light in a fading gilt box on a peeling plaster wall that people nod to as they pass? What does someone infer about God when they sit largely in silence in an aggressively white-washed walled room, trying to attune themselves to the "inner light" or voice of God? What does someone infer about God when they attend a meeting where music is cranked up to the volume of a Led Zeppelin concert and our ears are bleeding as we attempt to join in singing tuneless songs with meaningless lyrics? What are we to infer about God from seeing a man wearing medieval clothing with lace and dangly bits, performing strange actions, without commentary, with his back to those watching, engulfed by clouds of nausea-inducing smoke, with the odd tingle of tiny bells, spouting words in a passionless voice, about the most significant event in history?

These externals do say something about our internal spiritual worship. The question we must ask is whether they say the right thing, whether they speak truth about who God is and how God is. We must ask whether what we have become accustomed to in our normal expression of worship, offers anything meaningful to God, and says anything meaningful about God.

Three people's worship has visibly, physically taught me much about God and a life given over to Him. The first was a student called Tanya. During her three years with us, I observed her frequently in worship. She did not need to be encouraged, or take time to "tune in" – she would immediately step into worship, her eyes closed, and her arms flung wide open, literally bent back, expressing her complete abandonment to God. The second was a professor, a medal-winning, world-class mathematician who every single week in worship, would fall on his knees – in complete surrender and humility, a genius who knew his place before God. The third was an elderly bishop, David Pytches, who, for every single time of worship during a two-week conference, would lie prostrate on the floor, for an extended period, not asleep but devoted in adoring worship to His God. All three worshipped, and their worship demonstrated something beyond the words. Their worship was symbolic, prophetic.

Her worship was a memorial to her

… wherever the gospel is proclaimed in the whole world, what she has done will be told in memory of her.[68]

This drama being played out in a house in Bethany anticipates the crucifixion of a carpenter on a hill outside Jerusalem. Jesus tells us, firstly, that this is *gospel* – it is good news, joyful, wonderful; news of a Saviour come, of sins forgiven, of heaven opened. Secondly, this is a *global* message that will be preached throughout the world.

Remarkably, Jesus wills that not only must this gospel go global, but when it does, this woman must be honoured! When it is preached, mention will be made of her. He does not want us to forget her! Jesus does not want us to forget this kind of

---

68 Mark 14:9.

worship. To understand the gospel is to understand Christ, and to understand what our hearts owe to the Son of God.

Mary, in some sense, fulfils a type, and serves as an illustration of true devotion, of discipleship, of worship. She serves as a type of faith, a type of a giver, a sinner who received the forgiveness of her sins. But is that all Jesus meant when he said this? I think perhaps not. I rather think Jesus was so blown away by her, that just as at the Oscars, when the stars are being honoured, they often name those who helped, so Jesus too wants her named and known, perhaps because she was the first to "really get it", really understand and fully respond to Jesus in the way we all ought to.

Mary had fully and rightly identified with Jesus; Jesus would fully identify with her. She had spoken of Christ; Christ would speak of her. She had done a beautiful thing to Jesus, and He would show the world how beautiful she was to Him. So Christ commands that whenever the gospel is preached, the story of this worshipper is told with His story – in memory of her. The fact that her story is found in all four Gospels shows that the authors took seriously Jesus' command to remember her. But have we honoured her? Have we imitated her? Have we understood the normative standard of the heart's right response to the living God that she exemplifies?

We are used to seeing memorials. In every town and city in Britain there are war memorials to soldiers who sacrificially gave their lives in the two World Wars. I love the Martyrs Memorial in Oxford, a monument still there 450 years after the event, set up to remind us of three Protestant leaders – Ridley, Latimer, and Cranmer – who laid their lives down for their Lord. It is a marker that honours them, and inspires others to follow in their line, in honouring the Lord. And Mary's worship is a memorial to her Jesus, and her Jesus wants a memorial to her, that others will imitate her example. This confronts us with a further challenge: will I imitate her worship?

What will your life's memorial be?

In conclusion

The Gospel authors Matthew and Mark tell us that Jesus said that whenever the gospel is preached, her actions will be remembered. Luke adds Christ's comment: "her sins, which are many, are forgiven... . And he said to the woman, 'Your faith has saved you; go in peace.'"

She brought faith, sacrifice, worship – she left forgiven, saved, and honoured.

God honours those who honour him. Give and it will be given to you. It is a promise of Christ that is so true of worship – as we give, we receive. Worship is our gift to God, but remarkably, it is a gift given that gives back!

Some time ago, I was challenged by Mary's act of giving herself to Christ, and demonstrated this by giving her most prized possession – a bottle of pure nard worth a year's wages! I asked myself as I prepared a talk on this: what would I be willing to give, break, pour over Christ? Some readers will know my hobby is collecting old fountain pens, and I thought perhaps I would simply break a rare pen as a kind of burnt or broken sacrifice. However, as I mused about this, I was reminded that the next day was our church auction to raise cash for our interns' trip to South Africa. I sensed the Lord say: "Auction a rare pen for Me and give the proceeds to the interns."

Initially, I thought of auctioning "the chance" for someone to choose a pen of their choice from my collection of 200 pens – but inside I feared they'd take one of the best, and so I was reluctant to do this. I thought I'd choose one I wouldn't miss. Then the Lord challenged me: this woman gave everything – she gave her all for Him. So I decided to auction the rarest pen I then owned, a 1930s button-filling Conway Stewart in tan rubber. Not worth a year's wages, perhaps not even a month's, but rare, and one of only two or three known to exist in world. By the time I went to bed I'd talked myself into giving a lesser gift, but my wife Tiffany, a true worshipper, wouldn't allow it, and so I took the pen to the auction. Someone purchased it for a generous amount, and the money went to the interns' mission fund. I was pleased, not self-satisfied, but sensed God's pleasure that I had honoured him, however modestly, in giving away something that meant a lot to me. It was a genuine act of worship, albeit slightly hesitant, and without the generosity and abandon of the lady with the nard.

The next day was my birthday – I received a parcel. When I opened it, there was my pen, returned to me. I found out who had bought it and rang them up. I told them I didn't really want it back, as it was a gift given to God. But the person told me that when the item came up for sale, God had said to them: "Buy it and give it to Simon for his birthday." They had no idea it was my birthday the following day, but the next day they happened to see someone signing a birthday card for me, and so gave it that evening. I learnt a great deal from this – about true worship, costly worship, about friends who hear from God and give in love, and most of all about God who is *so* worthy of worship, of all we have, and yet who loves to give back to us out of His generous Father's heart.

Not long afterwards, a friend and former student, while visiting her father in Germany, saw an old pen in his desk drawer. Knowing her chaplain was a pen addict, she asked if she could have it to give to me. Her father freely agreed, adding that it was worth a few bob! With her husband she came for lunch, and just before dessert she said she had a present for me, and pulled a pen out of her pocket. When she gave it to me I nearly had a heart attack. I immediately knew what it was, though I had never seen one, not even in the definitive pen encyclopaedias. It was a 1930s Pelikan Toledo – among the rarest and most sought after of all vintage pens, worth almost as much as all my other 200 pens put together! It was a gift from her and her father, but I knew it was also a gift from God. No other object, no matter its value, could have spoken so powerfully to me, meant so much to me.

God honours those who honour him. We may never scale the dizzy heights of consecration shown by Mary, but no matter how paltry our offerings to God, He responds with lavish grace. We don't worship with any expectation to receive. Worship is one-way: we worship because God is worthy of it. And yet even as we lay down our crowns before Him, He graciously returns those crowns to us.

Chapter 4

Sing

HOLDING ON TO THE GIFT OF CORPORATE WORSHIP

Neil Bennetts

We all have our songs, our heart cries to God. We sing them in our cars, our homes, on the way to work. We sing them through pain and through joy. Sometimes they are audible and beautiful to the human ear. Often they may be silent, or lack musical expertise, but to God they are all treasured, and they are at the heart of the way He wishes to relate to His people. God Himself sings over us, and we sing back, responding as best we can to His overtures of love.

We sing when we are in love.

We sing when we need spurring on in our battles, our endeavours, our challenges. We sing when our hearts are breaking. We sing at the birth of our children, at the marriage of our families, and at the funerals of our loved ones. Songs help us celebrate our successes, express our intentions and grieve our losses. They give nations their identities and accompany their achievements.

Songs unite generations and peoples. They evoke memories of times gone by, of significant and wonderful events in our histories. They inspire us to dream and to travel the journey of life.

There is also power in the language of song.

Songs and the melodies and harmonies and rhythms that accompany them can evoke powerful and intense emotional reactions. The world knows this. A particular song can inspire someone to great acts of mercy, but can also compel someone to dreadful acts of depravity. A particular song can carry someone through great times of testing, but can also cause someone to give up. A particular song can capture our hearts to serve the broken people around us, but can also lure us to spend huge amounts of money we don't have on things we don't need.

Oh yes, when we are talking about singing, we are not talking about something that wanders around on the fringe of society, on the edges of people's lives. Singing is at the heart of this world and all that the world does.

But God is hungry for the sort of songs that express His goodness and His greatness back to Him in worship.

He is desperate for our praise.

He is listening out for our affection because He knows that if the song isn't sung to Him, it will be sung to someone else.

He calls loudly to all of the earth and all of heaven, "Come and sing to me!"

The psalmist says:

Praise the Lord.

Praise the Lord from the heavens, praise him in the heights above. Praise him, all his angels, praise him, all his heavenly hosts. Praise him, sun and moon, praise him, all you shining stars. Praise him, you highest heavens and you waters above the skies.

Let them praise the name of the Lord, for he commanded and they were created. He set them in place for ever and ever; he gave a decree that will never pass away.

Praise the Lord from the earth, you great sea creatures and all ocean depths, lightning and hail, snow and clouds, stormy winds that do his bidding, you mountains and all hills, fruit trees and all cedars, wild animals and all cattle, small creatures and flying birds, kings of the earth and all nations, you princes and all rulers on earth, young men and maidens, old men and children.

Let them praise the name of the Lord, for his name alone is exalted; his splendour is above the earth and the heavens.[69]

In the Bible, people sing to engage with spiritual and physical battles, they sing when they need God to break into seemingly impossible situations, they sing in their hunger to see God's presence tangibly invade their space, and they sing when they see God working His Kingdom out through them. Unsurprisingly, the longest book in the Bible is devoted to songs – their inspiration, their articulation, and their impact. It is, in fact, a songbook itself.[70] And the glorious events that will take place at the end of this age will unfold to a backdrop of song: earth and heaven joining together in a huge cacophony of praise.

Understanding the centrality of song to the Christian walk has inspired the church down the ages in its architecture. You only need to look at some of the great churches and cathedrals around the world to know that these were designed with singing in mind: the acoustics, the architecture, the later addition of massive organs, the choir stalls, the sound systems, all tend to be designed to facilitate singing. Furthermore, churches that throughout history have directed resources and time and effort into songs have been those generally which have been at the forefront of the advancement of the Kingdom, and great moves of God throughout history tend to be accompanied by the birth of new songs and new ways of expressing song. Songs seem to be both a herald to, and a consequence of, the advancement of God's Kingdom on earth.

69 Psalm 148:1–13.
70 The Psalms.

Enter one very awestruck worshipper.

If you are like me, you are totally amazed at the gift to us that song is, but you probably feel ill equipped to do it justice. When Charles Wesley wrote that incredible hymn, "O for a thousand tongues to sing my great Redeemer's praise", I wonder if this was what he was feeling. Such a great God to sing about, but such a sense of not having everything needed to do justice to this singing thing.

> *Who is like You, Lord of heaven, King of Glory,*
>   *clothed in majesty*
> *You are Holy, You are Holy*
> *Who can fathom all the riches of Your mercy, of Your*
>   *faithfulness*
> *You are worthy, You are worthy*
>
> *O for a thousand tongues to sing my Great*
>   *Redeemer's praise*
> *The honours of His Name*
> *Awake my soul and celebrate the wonders of His grace*
> *Let heaven and earth join in the song.*[71]

Stronger, louder, and more courageous: The special dynamic of corporate worship

If you are anything like me, you probably feel that your own singular voice tends to lack punch.

So often our individual songs can feel inadequate, our acts of praise can often seem isolated and faint. We know God's heart for song, we see the mark that singing leaves on the church and the world throughout history, we read the scriptures that have songs living and breathing though them, and we want to be part of it, but we often feel strangely limited in our ability to articulate

---

71 "Great Redeemer", Neil Bennetts, © 2004 Trinity Publishing. (It's a pale reflection of the original, but it says what I wanted to say.)

what we want to say to God, frustrated by the lack of colour in our words, disappointed by any sense of immediate impact in the Kingdom.

Yes, however precious to God our own individual voices are – and we must know that they are – we long to be part of the greater song, the song that has been so much part of the life of the church before us, and the life of the church yet to come. That is why, since the birth of the church, worshippers have sought each other out. We find that when our individual heart cries come together, when our personal descriptions of God's character as He has revealed Himself to us combine, they produce something altogether stronger, louder, and more courageous: we find that the combined resonance of many voices is thrilling, engaging, and encouraging.

Some time ago, I was enjoying being part of the congregation in church, loving the worship being led by one of my team, excited by hearing the passion and enthusiasm of the worshippers around me, and through it all, encountering God myself as I sang. Then just for a few moments I stopped singing. Out of the combined sound of the 500 or so singers that were there that evening, I began to hear some individual songs stand out.

Behind me to my right I heard someone proclaiming God's power and glory. Just behind me on the other side I sensed a more painful cry, a lament of someone struggling through difficulty. Another voice seemed to be pouring out pure love and devotion to Jesus. They were all singing roughly the same words, and nearly the same tune, but the different heart cries of those individual voices shone through, and it was as though a bigger, more glorious, more beautiful picture of God was being painted before my eyes. I found myself being urged on to sing louder, to lift my hands higher, to rejoice with more faith and maybe slightly more understanding.

I don't know what you think a worship leader is trying to do. For me, it is not so much about pushing the next great song, about performing to people, about speaking clever words over people, or getting good album sales, or impressing people with technical ability. For me, the primary role of the worship leader is to draw together all the individual voices and intentions in the room, to gather together all the heart cries of all the people present:

- those who are going through good times;
- those who are hurting;
- those who have just lost a loved one;
- those for whom the very act of opening their mouths to sing that day causes pain;
- those who have seen God work powerfully in their lives that week;
- those who feel God is a thousand miles away;
- those who are dealing with a terminal illness;
- those who are going through a relationship break-up;
- those who are struggling because they aren't married;
- those who are excited because they have just got married;
- those whose children are causing them pain;
- those who may have come to know Jesus that very day.

The role of the worship leader when they plug in their guitar and count in the band is to gather all those voices together, encouraging each one of them to contribute their own voice to the greater song of gathered praise, because whereas in isolation each one may express some small part of God's character, some small piece of the picture of who God is, gathered together they give a more glorious expression of His wonder and completeness: the Creator; the Eternal Father; the Faithful One; the Source of Life; the Comforter; the Healer; the Saviour; the Redeemer. And those individual voices that may have previously felt somewhat inadequate begin to find their strength.

One of the biggest challenges to the worship leader in this

current season is to press down on the pedal of accessibility. As musicians and artisans we love to develop our skill levels, but as soon as our pursuit of greater skill becomes more important than our capability to engage our congregations in song, then we have departed from our primary purpose. Elsewhere in this book we look at Bezalel – the artisan who was tasked with furnishing the tabernacle. He was someone with immense skill, but he also had understanding and knowledge. He wasn't chosen purely because of his gift, but also because of his wisdom: not only could he do amazing things, but he had developed the capability to work out if and when and where to do them – or not. I get sent many, many worship CDs to listen to. Most of them are full of great music and great songs that I just can't sing – tunes that are too complex, words that are too weird, ranges that are too great... Call me old fashioned, but isn't it time we recaptured the art of writing great songs that are easy to sing!

To be theological in our lyrics does not mean that we have to be long-winded; to be fresh in our musicality doesn't mean that we have to be complicated; to invoke emotion and passion doesn't mean we have to insist that our congregations have the vocal range of a hyena. If we as worship leaders are really serving our churches, we need to develop not only our skill, but also our wisdom so that we can be truly accessible.

I've often wondered what Paul means when he urges us to "Speak to one another with psalms, hymns and spiritual songs."[72] The thought of turning to my neighbour in church on a Sunday and singing some sort of cheesy "Jesus loves you" ditty leaves me cold. In fact, I remember singing a song, many years ago, which had the line, "Jesus stand among us at the meeting of our eyes", and being encouraged by the worship leader to look around at my mates in the congregation while I sang it.[73]

This sort of thing doesn't really work for me.

---

72 Ephesians 5:19.
73 For clarity – I don't dislike the song, only the way I was asked to sing it. I am an introvert, after all!

But what does work is finding my own feeble voice joining with many other feeble voices, and being encouraged and inspired and urged on in my worship. What does work for me is having my picture of God enlarged by the expressions of worship in the voices around me.

You see, God has gifted us with a wonderful thing called singing, and He has also gifted us with a context where we can be inspired and urged on in that singing, weaknesses and frailties included.

Of course, that context is church.

One of the hallmarks of our journey as the worldwide church over recent years has been the reawakening in us that worship is a way of life. It's become a slogan for many of us because we know that worship is much more than singing songs in church. It affects everything we do and say, the things we put our time and effort into, the relationships we have, the work we undertake.

Yes, worship is far more than singing songs.

But let's not forget, the singing bit is still important.

In our desire to broaden our understanding of worship as a lifestyle, let's not forget that coming to church and singing songs is still very important. "Let us not give up meeting together, as some are in the habit of doing, but let us encourage one another – and all the more as you see the Day approaching."[74]

Or as C. S. Lewis said: just as men spontaneously praise what they value, so they spontaneously urge others (i.e. us) to join them in praising it.

This marks us out: Being identified as God-worshippers

In AD 110 a man called Pliny the Younger was appointed the governor of the Roman province of Bithynia. His appointment came during a time of great persecution for the early church. Peter and Paul had both lost their lives under persecution some

74 Hebrews 10:25.

fifty years previously at the hand of the Emperor of the time – Nero – and since then Christians had been systematically interrogated, abused, tortured and executed for their faith by the Romans. But despite all of that, the church was growing.

Pliny the Younger wrote a series of letters to another Roman Emperor – Trajan – in AD 111, asking for advice on how to deal with what he described as a "contagion of superstition" spreading across his region. He was referring to the continued growth and multiplication of the Christian church.

In these letters he describes how he had continued to interrogate, violate, and execute many of the Christians in his province, and his frustration at failing to quench their multiplication and growth. He also indicated that the only thing cited as the conclusive evidence for their faith and loyalty to Jesus above the emperor was not what they believed, but what they did.

He said that "in the case of those who are accused to be as Christians, the sum total of their guilt or error is that they met regularly before dawn on a fixed day to chant verses amongst themselves in honour of Christ, as to a God."[75]

It was their gathered, sung worship that marked them out as followers of Jesus. It was their involvement in gathered sung worship that, in the eyes of the Romans, conclusively identified them as followers of Jesus and, in many cases, convicted them.

What a challenge this story is to many of us today who find it an effort to get to church on a Sunday because it messes up our Sunday-roast lunchtime routine.

When people open their mouths and sing songs of worship and honour to God, they not only encourage the saints around them, but they mark themselves out as followers of Jesus and attract the attention of the world around them in a way that other things don't.

It is interesting that in the UK (where I live) one of the most enduring and long-lasting programmes on TV is one called *Songs*

75 www.earlychristianwritings.com/text/pliny

of Praise; and it is amazing how many people who would never step into a church building will watch it. I remember appearing on the programme many years ago in a small capacity alongside a much more famous, higher-profile worship leader. The day after, when I went into the office where I worked in the insurance industry, I was amazed by the number of people who I would count amongst the least likely to engage with anything spiritual, who had watched it, seen me, and wanted to talk about it.

I also remember many years ago one of our daughters was being dedicated in church, and for that service we invited our National Childbirth Trust[76] group to be there – many of whom were not Christians. As we had the dedication part of the service, and had the talk and prayers, I felt reasonably comfortable sitting there alongside them. But when the band struck up and we all began singing, I suddenly felt somewhat different. Slightly self-conscious, if I am honest. In that moment, I felt that this act – the singing – was the most conclusive evidence to them that this thing was real for me.

Flung into the Father's arms: Lament in worship

I was sitting in a room with some worship leaders a few months ago in London, and the worship leader who was speaking at the sessions played us a muffled recording of a few people singing. Now there is nothing particularly unusual about that. However, it was the story that surrounded that recording that made it one of the most beautiful sounds I have ever heard.

The recording was made by a reporter friend of this worship leader who had been to a country where the Christians were being persecuted for their faith in a very violent manner. Their wives and children were being repeatedly raped and beaten.

---

76 NCT is an organization that brings expectant families together to share on the journey of childbirth. We are still friends with this group of people some fourteen years later.

Some of the men themselves had had their genitals cut away to stop them being able to father any more children who might perpetuate the faith. This reporter witnessed evidence of some of the most horrendous acts imaginable by one man to another. Even travelling to this small community of Christians was an incredibly dangerous journey for him.

When he arrived at this village he heard some people singing in the distance and he moved towards the sound. He eventually entered a building where a small group of Christian men were gathered, and he found them worshipping.

Singing songs to God.

Here were these men who had suffered abuse and torture and death in their families – and they were singing. The only thing this reporter had available to him was his mobile phone, and he managed to get a short sound-clip of their songs as they poured out their worship to God.

That is what we were listening to that day in London.

Not the latest worship song, recorded with a huge budget and amazing musicians and cleverly marketed around the world. But the muffled, imperfect song of a few faithful men, worshipping God amidst their troubled and painful circumstances. Circumstances that you or I probably never even imagine that we will have to contend with. The most amazing thing was that, although you could clearly sense the pain and fear in their singing, you could also sense the reality of their hope.

That is what made it such a beautiful sound.

There has been much discussion in worship circles recently about the whole area of lament in worship. It has been helpful, because all too often the church slips into a sort of "victorious living" type of mentality where doubt is frowned upon, or where we are encouraged to leave our problems at the entrance of the church when we arrive.

Some of the early songs we used to sing as worship leaders

in the eighties used all sorts of unhelpful language. I seem to remember an old song that we used to sing that encouraged us to forget about ourselves as we worshipped, or another song that suggested that all our problems disappeared when we sang songs. Whereas the intention may have been good, quite often the theology was bad, and I think people and churches were damaged by it. So there has been a real need to revisit this whole area.

Kenny Borthwick, a friend of mine who leads a church in Edinburgh, came to speak at a conference I was running. As he spoke, he talked of the time when a young lady in his congregation, who had a history of self-harming, walked out of the church during one of the services, cut her leg with a piece of glass, and then walked back into church, with blood pouring from her wound. He realized there was clearly something that this young lady had managed to learn about church – that you leave your struggles at the door when you enter for worship. She had taken this message to heart, and had gone back outside the door to attend to her problems before coming back into the building to carry on with worship.

Kenny said that it changed his whole attitude to worship, and that since that day he had come to understand that when we worship, rather than leave the undesirable or painful parts of us at the door, or ignore our challenges and fears as we sing, we should bring all of ourselves to all of God.

All of ourselves – our struggles, our achievements, our sicknesses, our disappointments, our frustrations, our successes, our difficult relationships, our testing children, our money worries, our promotions – all of us, to all of God – His goodness, His faithfulness, His mystery, His majesty, His nearness, and His otherness – even those parts of Him and His dealings with us that are utterly inexplicable.

We bring all of ourselves, to all of God, when we worship.

After the conference, as we were chatting, I thanked Kenny

for his talk, and told him that it had helped articulate something that I had been sensing for some time – that in our desire to address a weakness or even error in the way we understood the place of lament in worship in our churches, I felt we had appeared to have got to a point where we were actually glorifying lament. Various songwriters, theologians, and church leaders had written on the subject in a well-intentioned desire to address the issue, but I was sensing that it was getting to the stage that our worship was being judged on its lament content, and that our songwriters were being unduly pressurized to write songs about lament. There seemed to be a general thought going round that if we sang more lament songs, our worship would somehow be transformed.

Kenny then said something else that was extremely helpful – he said that the pain we bring in worship should never be exalted above its ability to fling us into the Father's arms.

Lament is real, but it is not something to which we should aspire. It is a natural part of a broken church being full of broken people from a broken world, but it is not something that we should glorify beyond its ability to fling us into the embrace of God. Being able to come into a community gathered in worship and be able to express the pain and disappointment you are feeling in life is a real gift – and at the centre of that gift is the way that as we sing with such feeling, we know God sings over us, and somehow we are drawn into His loving arms where, in a very real way, He lifts our heads. But conversely, if we come to church and worship and we don't find ourselves burdened with pain or suffering or disappointment, then I don't think we should look for it, or, even worse, feel somehow inadequate or incomplete because we're not feeling that way.

Depending on a person's particular emphasis or context or life circumstances, the Psalms are either viewed primarily as songs of praise, or primarily as songs of lament. It seems to me, though, that they consist of lament and praise, all beautifully entwined in acts of worship. Praise follows lament follows praise follows lament. It seems that the psalmist could not separate his brokenness and troubles from his thankfulness and wonder of God.

As I've been reflecting on all of this, I have come to the conclusion that there is something that seems to wrap itself around our songs – something that allows lament and joy to combine together in songs of real authenticity and community – and that is hope. It seems that whatever place we find ourselves in, we are able to join together in songs of amazing hope. Hope is the great leveller for all of us who gather together and sing – whether that is in the midst of persecution, pain, rejoicing or celebration, and so it is to the songs of hope that I now need to turn our attention.

Left breathless: Hope in worship

I was cycling into work early one morning and I had a tune going round in my head.

A few weeks earlier I had been asked to write a song for Naomi House in my home county of Hampshire. Naomi House is a place that cares for terminally ill children, and my mother worked there for a while on a volunteer basis. They were celebrating their tenth anniversary in Winchester Cathedral and had asked if I would write a song for the event. Of course I said "yes", but after agreeing to do it, I began to panic a little. What would be an appropriate thing to ask a team of carers and the people they care for (many of whom could well be facing their final days on earth) to sing? What could I ask of a bunch of people who were seeing life ebb away from them – people who had been dealing with the confusing possibility that a loving God would allow their sickness to overcome their life?

Then as I cycled that day, I realized that there was one thing that those children have, that all of us have.

Hope.

The song that finally came out of that time was called "O Perfect Love", the third verse of which goes like this:

O perfect love, forever I shall sing
Of heaven's gates flung wide for me.
Where fear of death and tears of hopelessness
Are swallowed up in victory.
And what praise shall be sung still to the Holy One
To the Saviour, Redeemer and King
O perfect love
My song will ever be "I am found in Jesus."[77]

Then I saw a new heaven and a new earth, for the first heaven and the first earth had passed away, and there was no longer any sea. I saw the Holy City, the new Jerusalem, coming down out of heaven from God, prepared as a bride beautifully dressed for her husband. And I heard a loud voice from the throne saying, "Now the dwelling of God is with men, and he will live with them. They will be his people, and God himself will be with them and be their God. He will wipe every tear from their eyes. There will be no more death or mourning or crying or pain, for the old order of things has passed away. He who was seated on the throne said, "I am making everything new!" Then he said, "Write this down, for these words are trustworthy and true."[78]

There probably aren't many of us who at some time or another haven't been moved to tears by this passage. It's ironic, really – that a passage that so eloquently describes a time when our tears will cease is also a passage that causes them to flow. The promise of a time when we shall stand before the throne of God,

77 "O Perfect Love", Neil Bennetts, © 2004 Kingsway Music.
78 Revelation 21:1–5.

perfect in His eyes, joined with the saints down the generations, worshipping the perfect Father of all creation in a place that is so beautiful and so full of God's light, that even the sun itself will not need to shine any more[79] – this is a wonderful picture of hope that captures our souls, fires our hearts and leaves us breathless.

> Then the angel showed me the river of the water of life, as clear as crystal, flowing from the throne of God and of the Lamb down the middle of the great street of the city. On each side of the river stood the tree of life, bearing twelve crops of fruit, yielding its fruit every month. And the leaves of the tree are for the healing of the nations. No longer will there be any curse. The throne of God and of the Lamb will be in the city, and his servants will serve him. They will see his face, and his name will be on their foreheads. There will be no more night. They will not need the light of a lamp or the light of the sun, for the Lord God will give them light. And they will reign for ever and ever.[80]

Ezekiel saw that this river would flow.[81]

He described it as a river that would make the salt water fresh again, that would be the source of life and fruitfulness for all who drank of it. A river that would bring healing and wholeness, that would unite peoples and nations. It is a picture of our future existence and dwelling with God that we rightfully hold on to through the disappointments of this life. It is a picture of total transformation, when all will be laughter and all will be praise, when we will perpetually drink from the river of life that will sustain us, enliven us, fulfil us.

This is our hope.

On that day we will join with people from every tongue,

---

79 Revelation 21:23.
80 Revelation 22:1–5.
81 Ezekiel 47:1–12.

tribe, and nation.[82] There will be so many people gathered around the throne that it will be impossible to count them. The barriers that have divided us in this life, the unhelpful labels that society places upon us, will be replaced by the reflection of God Himself upon our foreheads.

We will be marked with the mark of God Himself.

This mark won't be something that causes us to be unidentifiable or indistinguishable or insignificant, but it will be a mark that unites us together as people with a common inheritance as sons and daughters of the living God Himself. Even the angels – those heavenly beings that we seldom see in this life, but who we know have been so near us throughout our earthly journey – will become fully visible. They will worship with us, and us with them, and between us we will sing heaven's eternal songs, anthems that we will never, never tire of.

There will be no flagging here. There will be no sense of the songs becoming stale, or over-used, or losing their creative edge. It will be a time of sustained, glorious, beautiful, captivating worship before a glorious, beautiful, captivating King.

"Holy, holy, holy is the Lord God Almighty, who was, and is, and is to come."[83] "Praise and glory and wisdom and thanks and honour and power and strength be to our God for ever and ever. Amen."[84]

The sounds and the tunes and the harmonies and the colours and the rhythms that will be seen and heard on that day will be the most incredible sounds, tunes, harmonies and colours and rhythms ever seen and heard. Their creativity will be so amazing that they will never cease to grab us, inspire us, and cause us to worship all the louder and stronger.

This is our hope.

No more tears. No more fear of death.

No more disappointments.

---

82 Revelation 7:9–12.
83 Revelation 4:8.
84 Revelation 7:12.

No more pain.

No more sickness.

No more friends who let us down.

No more husbands or wives being unfaithful.

No more of our children suffering through cancer.

No more broken promises, no more job losses, no more insecurity, no more power struggles.

No more elderly people being abused.

No more drug dealers ruling through fear on depressed council estates.

No more watching a loved one having to struggle with the debilitating effects of a degenerative condition.

No more bullying in the school playground.

No more pictures of starving, emaciated children on our TV screens.

No more homelessness or despair.

No more going through life with the scars of an abusive father or an absent mother.

Just colour, and life, and light, and laughter, and beauty, and wonder that never cease, never fade, never run out.

This is our hope.

We will one day gather around the throne and worship in this condition, and in this way.

Jesus will be the centre of it all.

It will be amazing.

The King has come: Hope breaking into our lives through worship

We are always tempted in life to put something or someone in the place of Jesus.

Even in worship.

But it seems to me that when we do that, we start to lose our hope because Jesus is the Hope of the World. Both He and the hope He embodies are with us today. Hope isn't just a picture of the future. It isn't something that remains a dream of one of the saints of old, hallucinating on some warm Greek island. The throne we will gather around on that day is the same throne we are invited to gather round today. It is the same throne, it has the same King sitting on it, and the light and the colour and the beauty and the life-giving river that flows from it, flows into our lives today.

Here.

Now.

The same throne. The same King. The same river.

The King has already come. He is already seated on the throne. He is already inspiring songs of immense praise. He is already welcoming people who stoop with the burdens that life has thrown upon them and He allows the light of His presence to shine on them. Although sometimes the throne can seem somewhat distant, it still shines its light and power into our everyday lives, leading us forward, and inspiring us to carry on, pursue justice, seek holiness. Although our view of the King can sometimes be distorted or incomplete because of our experiences and influences in this life, it is the same King whom we will see in complete perfection on that day.

The Jesus-King.

The Christ-King.

Centre of it all.

And the river is the same river. Although the path of the river may often seem winding and unclear as it navigates through the barriers in our lives, as it winds its way around the consequences of our disobedience, or the disobedience of those who came before us, it is the same river. It is already flowing, full of the promise of salvation, full of the goodness and faithfulness of a living God. And it is already flowing with power to change and impact the course of our lives.

The more I read Revelation, the last book in the Bible, the more I sense that it is the book that most helpfully sets the context for our worship today. The more I set my heart on the time to come at the end of this age, the more I find a reason to sing, a reason to worship, a reason to open my mouth, lift up my hands and honour God. So when people come to our church on Sunday, I am more convinced than ever that we need to be singing with hope, talking of hope, sharing our hope.

When we come to worship on a Sunday we need to be inviting people to drink of that river, that river that brings us life and energy and strength.

When people who have yet to come to know Jesus come into our church, most of all I want them to hear us singing about hope.

I believe this will grab people's hearts more than anything else we do.

He came so we could know the Father's love.
    The Saviour, the Healer.
He came to seek and save all that was lost,
    Restorer, Redeemer.
Light in the darkness, help to the helpless, a song for
    those who mourn
Strength for the weary, friend to the lonely, the joy of the
    whole earth.

The King has come, the glorious the awesome
    Son of God
The beautiful the sovereign Lord of love, Jesus.
The King has come, and everything within this
    heart believes
That He is everything we'll ever need: Jesus the
    King has come.

He came to bring the message of new birth. The creator,
    sustainer.
He came to bring His rule upon the earth with justice
    and mercy.

*And His ways are higher, His love is greater than the
   treasures of this world
His grace is wider, His name is stronger. He's the joy of
   the whole earth.*

*This is the time this is the place, let the Kingdom of our
   God reign.*[85]

Holding on to the gift of gathered, sung worship: Keeping it central

Worship is our highest calling and our ultimate destination. And at this point in history, at the beginning of the twenty-first century, I think one of the biggest challenges to the Western church is not that it won't be able to devise programmes of evangelism, that it won't be able to run mercy ministries to the poor, or that it won't be able to find its political voice in our nations. Its biggest challenge is to hold on to the wonder of, experience the life-changing power of, and devote itself passionately to its gathered, sung worship.

I recently gave a talk for a group of theological students on worship, and at the end of the session I presented them with the words of the last paragraph. I am not sure they understood or agreed with me, judging by the looks on their faces.

However, despite the questioning looks from those students, I passionately believe it, because I have sensed an increasing tendency for followers of Jesus – especially in the West – to put church and worship increasingly lower on their list of priorities. I have sensed more and more authors and churchpeople – especially those that would describe themselves as being from the emergent church – down-playing the centrality of gathered worship in the life of the church. Some will even say that people don't gather to worship very often because "they are doing church

---

85 "The King Has Come", Neil Bennetts and Eoghan Heaslip, © 2008 Trinity Publishing/Thankyou Music.

differently these days". To which I want to respond: "Then maybe they are doing church wrong."

A few weeks after giving that talk, I was reading a book from a very well-known author, whose books sell in massive quantities worldwide. In one of the opening chapters he essentially said that if church wasn't working for you, then maybe you should stop going.

Church attendance in the West is falling. Much of that is because more and more people are deserting faith, but some of the decline, I suspect, is that people of faith are deserting a church that has lost its passion for gathered, sung worship.

I am the first to admit that in some ways, the church has lost its way in worship in recent years. We've become a little too focused on industry and profile and celebrity and money. We've all too often painted church and worship as a gathering of perfect people singing perfect songs in a perfect auditorium with no pain or disappointment in sight. We've becoming increasingly skilful and intricate while becoming less and less accessible to both the church and those we are trying to reach. We've used excellence to cover up a lack of creativity and wonder, and in all of this we have maybe started to lose touch with the very essence of worship itself.

But it seems to me that the answer isn't to reject church and gathered, sung worship. The answer is to rediscover the wonder of it, and devote ourselves more fully to it: this life-giving, soul-satisfying, hope-inspiring, God-honouring, battle-winning, church-strengthening gift called singing.

Chapter 5

Love and Loved

A LOVING RESPONSE TO BEING LOVED BY GOD

Simon Ponsonby

True worship is loving God who first loved us

The psalmist repeatedly employed the refrain "His love endures forever." Celebrating the love of God was a key theme in Israel's worship and praise. The exact phrase "His love endures forever" occurs over forty times in the Bible, notably as the opening line of Psalms 106 and 107, and in Psalm 136 it is repeated no less than twenty-six times, being the explanation to every statement of God's creative and redemptive acts. It is the motivation, the conclusion and the presupposition to everything God is and everything He has done in creation and redemption history. And as such, it is the single most repeated phrase in Israel's worship book, the Psalms. The God who has loved us is the God who invites, woos and even commands us to love Him.

In the good but slightly gushing movie *Notting Hill*, Hugh Grant plays William, a poor, divorced, failed bookseller who strikes up a strained romance with Anna, the world's most famous actress, played by Julia Roberts. The film is about how these two unlikely matched people fall in love and eventually marry. Towards the end of the film, Anna comes to the bookshop and asks William if there is any future in their relationship.

William says no: "I live in Notting Hill and you live in Beverly Hills. Everyone in the world knows who you are – my mother has trouble remembering my name." Then Anna touchingly dismisses the obstacles and replies, "I'm also just a girl, standing in front of a boy, asking him to love her."

Far-fetched film fantasy!

And yet God, the one and only, the Lord and Creator and Sustainer of the universe, who dwells in unapproachable light, who has no beginning nor end, who is omnipotent, omniscient, omnipresent, before whom the angels worship, and the sun, moon and stars bow down – the whole of creation hangs by His breath – that God invites us not just to be His followers, but stands before us asking us to be His lovers.

When I went to theological college to train for the Anglican ministry, my very first assignment was to write a detailed study of the Greek text of John 21:15f, paying particular attention to the subtle differentiations between John's use of paired words: sheep and lambs (*probaton* and *arnia*); tending (*boskein* and *poimainein*) and love (*agape* and *phileo*). I think I got so bogged down in the subtleties in the text, I missed the point. I failed to see the wood for the trees. I was so intrigued by the subtle nuances of the Greek language that I missed the message.

I am a passionate photographer. But some photographic commentators spend all their time "counting pixels" – studying photos to see how much chromatic aberration or edge-blurring or "noise" there is, and failing completely to study the image and composition! I think theological scholarship can often be like this.

Flush or wash

John 21 is the first proper conversation between Peter and Jesus since the night Jesus was betrayed by Judas, arrested by the religious authorities and abandoned by His disciples. That night Peter, just as Jesus had prophesied, denied knowing and following Jesus three times.

In this passage, the resurrected Jesus meets the disciples

back at Galilee, and after giving them a hearty breakfast, takes Peter on a walk along the shore, and here in the very place where Peter first encountered Jesus, forsaking all to follow Him, Jesus confronts Peter's threefold denial, and seeks to restore Peter through inviting a threefold affirmation of love. Each affirmation of love receives a recommissioning of Peter to apostolic service. Jesus gives Peter an opportunity to undo, erase, recant, repent, and be restored. Jesus wants forgiveness, not failure, to mark Peter's life from now on. Jesus could have started again, found another leader – I would have! But He would rather restore Peter than replace him!

A while ago, I was teaching at a church leaders' conference and, in part, addressing the themes of grace. One evening, while I was paying a visit to the loo, my signet ring slipped off and fell in the toilet. Unfortunately, I had just done the business and my ring was buried in the day's detritus! I was confronted with a choice: either to flush my ring away and claim insurance and buy another one, or to reach into the mess and rescue my ring.

Well, it meant too much to flush away!

And so I reached in, unable to see it, rummaged around in the mess until I found it – and then nearly developed OCD as I scrubbed my ring and my arm with disinfectant (for half an hour)!

Christ had the choice to flush Peter away in his sin, or to reach in, and rescue, and clean, and reappoint. And as we shall see, Jesus chose to restore Peter – it is that experience of grace which would lead Peter to live a laid-down life of worship and service, as he would later write: "To him be the glory both now and to the day of eternity."[86]

Do you love Me?

Three times Peter denied Jesus, three times Jesus elicits a profession of devotion. Before Peter can face the future, Jesus

---

86 2 Peter 3:18.

needs to deal with and heal the past. Each time Peter responds, "Yes, I love you", it's as if the thorn placed by denial into Peter's soul is removed. Peter's threefold denial is not the last word – God's grace makes space for new words, tender words, restoring words, loving words. Jesus asks him, "*Agapas* me."

Of course, the evidence is that Peter doesn't. This superlative of loves, this *agape* love, is the love Jesus shows at Calvary, the love which "lays down one's life for one's friends".

But Peter denied Jesus.

It was patently evident he didn't love Jesus with this love. Peter can only reply with a lesser, lighter-weight love (Greek: *phileo*) – a brotherly, family love. He can't measure up to the self-sacrificing *agape* love which Jesus showed and is owed. Perhaps we never can! But remarkably, it's enough. Jesus doesn't expect from us what He gives to us. He knows of what we are made. And each time Peter replies in the affirmative, albeit with diminutive love, Jesus kisses him with a commission: "Simon, do you love me?" is followed by "Simon, feed my sheep. Simon tend my lambs."

Maybe some reading this can identify with Peter.

You have really messed up.

You have known the Lord's presence, intimacy, call, and yet under pressure of temptation or trial you have denied Him, failed Him. Maybe even three times – "three" being a Semitic idiom, a figure of speech meaning "totally, fully, completely".

Maybe you have really blown it with the Lord.

But grace triumphs. Grace truly triumphs. The evil one wants accusation and condemnation to be the final word over our lives – but grace makes way for restoration, for recommission.

One of the world's great modern gurus of church growth has recently offered as a key axiom for leadership: rewarding high performers and removing under-performers. In many ways this makes perfect sense – invest in who and what is working, not who and what isn't. Don't waste time on wasters. And one might even find certain biblical texts to support such a view, notably the parable of the talents. But here in this narrative of Peter's restoration and recommission, Jesus employs the opposite. Jesus rewards this under-performer. The leader who has proven unfaithful and unreliable, who denies Jesus not once, not twice, but three times in as many hours – this fickle, faithless follower is made head of the church.

Peter, who knew the power of Christ's forgiveness, having denied Jesus three times, yet been restored to apostleship, later wrote, "Love covers a multitude of sins" – God's love for us and our love for God. Sin and failure He can deal with – it's only the absence of any turning to God in love which brings exclusion and ultimate rejection, leaving us to ourselves and our sin. What stands out starkly here is that love for God is the primary criterion for leadership, for apostleship, for discipleship.

Jesus didn't go to hell and back to make us His slaves. Love redeemed us to be lovers.

The biblical professor Leon Morris once wrote: "Loving Jesus is the fundamental qualification for service. Other qualities may be desirable, this love is indispensable."

Sadly, church is full of people who want to feed sheep, but who don't love the Shepherd. There are countless clergy who can barely mutter the Creed without perjury, and who know nothing of Calvary love and love for Calvary. I have met them – ministers who love the ministry, but don't know the Master. Theologians who love theology but don't love Theos. One only has to think of the numerous clergy and ministers who are also members of the atheist organization "Sea of Faith" to illustrate the point. Its website speaks of such unbelieving ministers refusing to abandon the church to fundamentalists – meaning believers!

In the process for becoming ordained, I must have been through a dozen interviews, assessing my suitability for the ministry. Intelligence, vocation, psychological profile, emotional stability, marriage, gifting, personal story – all these were put under the scrutiny of examining chaplains. But not once was I ever asked, "Do you love Jesus?" The sublime Anglican Ordination service, with its questions and answers asked publicly of those being ordained, never asks whether they love Jesus.

Jesus didn't ask Peter: "Have you got a good degree, good pedigree? Do you look good in a cassock? Have you done a Myers Briggs psychological profile or a Belbin analysis on team functions?" He asked him if he loved Him.

The most effective disciple is not the most educated, most gifted, best connected, but the most passionate about Jesus, the one who glows and overflows with love for Jesus. Nothing is more attractive or effective than a saint in love with her or his Saviour. Passion breeds passion, indifference breeds indifference. For centuries Christians have devoured and been inspired by the passion for Jesus shown in that remarkable Puritan warrior, Samuel Rutherford. Imprisoned for his faith in Scotland, he would often preface his letters, "From Christ's palace in Aberdeen" – so intense and beautiful were his times of intimacy with Jesus in his cell. In one letter he writes: "I don't know which person of the Trinity I love more – I know this, I love each of them and need them all."

It is well known that the Welsh Revival began in early 1904 in West Wales and was indebted to the preparatory prayers and ministry of Evan Roberts. What is less well known is that the revival broke out after an incident with a young girl called Florie Evans. One Sunday, at the end of the service, she went to her pastor, the Revd Jenkins, for spiritual counsel: "I long for spiritual joy and peace." He simply replied, "Surrender to the lordship of Christ, submit to the leading of the Holy Spirit."

She spent the next few days doing that, praying and consecrating her whole being to Christ as Lord.

And God visited her.

A couple of weeks later, she asked to give testimony at her church, and she stood up and merely said, "I love Jesus with all my heart." People wept. God came upon that congregation and God's Spirit swept through that country. The church was renewed, the community was transformed, and an estimated 100,000 converts were added to the church in just six months.

It's strange but true – the one thing Jesus asks for, the one thing Jesus is looking for is Peter's love. The Dutch theologian, Abraham Kuyper once wrote: "Even the heart of God thirsts after love." The first and greatest commandment – on which all the others hang, on which all the others are mere commentary – is not a prohibition, not a "thou shalt not". It's an affection, invitation, embrace, welcome, longing for intimacy: "Love the Lord your God with all your heart and with all your soul and with all your might."[87] This is what God wants of us. He wants *us* – he wants us to love Him. "Simon, do you love me?" is the question that confronts us all. True worship is loving Christ and loving Christ is true worship – in word and deed and life, poured out in obedience.

If loving God is the Great Commandment, then the Great Transgression is *not* loving God.

The French existentialist writer Albert Camus once wrote that the love of God is a hard love: it demands total surrender. And total surrender is what Peter would give. When he repeated his third affirmation, "You know that I love you", Jesus proceeded to tell him that just as he was dressed and led by others as a child, so he would be tied and led by others where he did not want to go as an old man (verses 18–19). This was a prophecy that indicated Peter's eventual arrest and death as a martyr. Refusing to deny Christ, he would be crucified upside down during the reign of Emperor Nero.

Peter had denied Christ, but he would eventually die for Christ.

And it was his love for Christ that would be the cause of both his death and his willingness to endure it. No doubt the breathtaking love of God for him, experienced in part by Jesus' forgiveness and restoration and commissioning of Peter, would

87 Deuteronomy 6:5.

not permit him to deny his Saviour again. Even in death, Peter's love for Jesus would drive him to offer his life as a sacrifice of worship to the one who loved and forgave and restored him.

Jesus asks: "Simon, do you love me?"

It is easy for me to identify with that sentence – Simon is my name. I read it as if our Lord is addressing it directly to me. But we all need to put our name in the place of Simon – for Jesus addresses us too:

"John, do you love me? Anna, do you love me? Michael, do you love me? Francis, do you love me? Vanessa, do you love me? Will, do you love me? Amanda, do you love me? Andrea, do you love me? Justin, do you love me?"

And worship is a life and a song and a gift that says, "Yes, Lord, you know that I love you – not as much as you love me, but I do."

We all know that sometimes love grows cold.

Jesus warned that this would be the mark of many in the last days – temptations and trials would cool their ardour for Christ. Jesus, in a message to the Ephesian church, commended them for many things, but said He had one thing against them: "You've lost your first love." Even as some marriages grow cold, stale, dull – people losing their appetite and affection for each other – so sometimes our relationship with God seems to lose its lustre, even its love.

Maybe you allowed a moon to eclipse between you and Jesus – demands of career, studies, relationships, family, hobbies, the pressures of life and the cares of this world just caused that passion for Jesus to dissipate and turn your faith into religion, joy into duty? It is good to ask ourselves: Was there ever a time when Jesus was nearer and dearer to me? And if so, what happened?

Shakespeare's Othello said to Desdemona: "When I love thee not – chaos is come again." When we love God, life begins to be put in order.

We are made to love God.

It's in our DNA, it's our destiny.

Only when we love God are we ourselves, fully alive, fully human. We find ourselves by losing ourselves in loving Jesus.

The night before I wrote this, after my son Joel went to bed, he sent me a text message on his mobile phone. It just said: "I love you over the moon and back and again, for infinity." A father can take any amount of messy bedrooms, Lego left hanging around. My son's free declaration of love makes my life worth living.

When was the last time you told the Lord you love Him? Worship is part of our expression of love to God. Worship is orientating our affections for God to God.

It is lovers' speech, and the more we experience the grace of God given to us in Christ, the more we will worship.

Do you know Jesus loves you?

Our love is a response to Christ's love for us – our worship is a response to the God who has graced us with worth. St John wrote, "We love [Jesus] because he first loved us."[88]

Our love is response, it is second order – His love is *a priori*, the love of the one who knew us before we were formed. Truly, love takes the initiative.

The Danish philosopher and prophet, Søren Kierkegaard, wrote: "You loved us first, O God... If I rise at dawn and in the very first second of my awakening my soul turns to You in prayer, You have beat me to it; You have already turned in love toward me."[89] As a bowed sunflower lifts its head and turns to the warmth of the rising sun, so this love of Christ causes our hearts to open towards Him in worship.

In John 21:20 "Peter turned and saw the disciple whom Jesus loved following them, the one who had been reclining at table close to him."

---

88 1 John 4:19.
89 Taken from George K. Bowers (ed.), *Søren Kierkegaard: The Mystique Of Prayer and Pray-er,* Css Pub Co, 1995, p. 27.

I confess I have often been troubled by this phrase, "The disciple whom Jesus loved," which John uses to describe himself six times in his Gospel. I felt that it implied a "favouritism", that Jesus indeed had His golden boys, His preferred, chosen, select, in-crowd. And I guess deep down I felt excluded from that inner core, on the outside, never quite making it in. And in this false sense of rejection, I also became resentful of those who appeared to be in. I readily identified with Peter, especially in his impetuous behaviour, his zeal without wisdom, and his bravado wed to failure. But John – well, John I didn't connect to, whether in his depiction in the Gospels or in his epistles.

This resentment of the "beloved disciple" was really jealousy. I reckoned that John was the sort to wear a T-shirt stating: "Jesus loves you but I'm His favourite." This deep sense of rejection affected my faith, my perception of others, and of God. It affected my worship, my devotion. I unconsciously reasoned that if Jesus had favourites like John, special "beloveds", then maybe I could graduate to this inner core and be a "beloved disciple". I knew I was justified by grace through faith… but could I get promoted? I wondered if perhaps by spending longer in my quiet times, perhaps by working harder at my faith-sharing, perhaps by giving more than my tithe, such effort would impress the Lord and improve my ranking.

As a young minister, I once asked the milkman (yes, there was a time when milk was delivered to the door before breakfast) what time he started his work. He told me 4:00 a.m. I reasoned that I worked for God, and I ought to be the first person at work in the town, not the milkman – and so I used to get up at 3:30 a.m. and spend the next five hours before breakfast praying, studying and snoring.

I wanted Jesus to take notice of me, and say "Son, come up higher." This wasn't just the zeal of youth, it was a longing to be a beloved disciple. I hoped that if I prayed harder than others, studied harder than others, gave harder than others, worshipped harder than others, then maybe God would love me more than others. But I was wrong. Worship is not a work. Worship is not a manipulation to wring more out of God.

True worship is not for gain.

True worship is not seeking to get noticed by God or promoted by God. We don't worship to get something, we worship to give something to the God who gave up His life for us.

If our faith isn't grounded in being loved, it will be grounded in legalism. Many, not understanding that we are loved, strive and strain to gain favour. I simply failed to understand that He already loved me as much as He could. He had no more love to give, for He had already directed all of it to me at Calvary.

Unless we know the Father's love, we tend towards the older brother in the parable of the prodigal son: we cannot enjoy the party, we resent the Father's grace to our brothers and sisters. We can even resent God – "All these years I've slaved for you and you've never given me 'n' my pals a goat!" – and we can't hear the Father crying, "My son, all I have is yours!"

Then, one day, when I was a new chaplain in Oxford, I read John speaking of himself as "the beloved disciple" and I could feel the bile rising, the rejection, the resentments – and then God spoke to me. Deep into my mind and spirit words came: "Simon, I don't love John any more than I love you. The only difference is, that he knows he is loved!" I broke into tears, deep wells opened up within me as God's love poured in and my rejection poured out.

I knew it was true.

Later Jesus revealed to me: "On the night that I was betrayed, John leant on my breast not because he was my favourite, but because he understood he was welcome – they all were, even Judas – but only he came and rested." And we see that the first one leaning is the last one standing – the only one who entered into that intimacy with Jesus is the only one of the twelve standing at Calvary.

John's self-title "the beloved disciple" was not arrogance, it was assurance. John didn't call himself "beloved disciple" because he thought he was loved any more than others, but simply because he knew he was loved. His identity was secure in the affections of Christ. That day, the conservative in me wanted to test what I sensed God revealing to me. "How do I know this is true? How do I know I too am a beloved disciple?"

The Lord immediately directed me to the Greek text of 1 John, one of John the beloved's pastoral letters to the church. Here, when addressing the believers, six times he uses the same title for each of them in the plural that he used of himself – they are *agapetoi*, the "deeply beloved" (1 John 2:7; 3:2, 21; 4:1, 7, 11). The NIV translates this as "dear friends". That's plain wrong – that would be the Greek word *philoi*. No, John is very clear – the description he uses for himself is the description he applies to the church – he, and we, are deeply beloved disciples.

Even when, like Peter, we may only love Jesus with a lesser love – *philo* – He is always the God who loves us with *agape*.

It is often said, but less often understood or believed, that God "so loved the world that he gave his only begotten Son". We know the verses: "greater love has no man than this, than he lay down his life for his friend", and yet do we believe it?

Listen, Jesus cannot love you any more than He already does. He has already loved us to death! Jesus is the only God the world has ever heard of who loves sinners. The medieval mystic Catherine of Siena, the first woman ever to be conferred the degree Doctor of Theology by the Catholic Church, often began her prayers by addressing God thus: "O Divine Madman". When asked why, she replied that God is *pazzo d'amore, ebro d'amore* – "crazy with love, drunk with love"! And we love because He first loved us; we worship because He first loved us.

So, how do we come to know this fierce love of God? We may meditate upon the objectivity of love laid down at Calvary; and we may experience the love subjectively by the internal witness of the Sprit. For it is the Spirit who sheds abroad the love of God in our hearts.90 The Holy Spirit unites us to God's love, and St Paul, knowing how desperately the church needs to experience this love, a love beyond knowing, prays that we may have more of the Spirit, that we will be "rooted and established in his love", and that we "may have power ... to grasp how wide and long and high and deep is the love of Christ", and that we may "know this love that surpasses knowledge".[91]

Judson Cornwall's brother Robert was a pastor in Oregon, USA. He had a poor income and looked to supplement it at the local hospital as a counsellor. The day he arrived they took him to Room 37. In this padded cell were thirty-seven drug-controlled psychotic patients – half-naked, in nappies, in hell.

The Lord said: "Sit on the floor."

Robert sat in the middle of the filth.

The Lord said to him: "Sing a song."

From deep within he began singing: "Yes, Jesus loves me, Yes, Jesus loves me – the Bible tells me so."

After an hour he was let out. A week later he returned to work and was taken back to Room 37. Again he sang this song. This time a large black woman, touched deep in her being, drawn by love, sat behind him and joined in the song. He kept this up every visit. Within a month thirty-six of the thirty-seven were on self-help wards; within a year thirty-five of them were out of hospital. Two became members of his church.

God sets our lives in order. Oh, how the church needs to know God's love!

That love which sets life in order.

That love which expands our heart for God, fuels our passion for worship and fills our language of praise.

Worship, true worship, is the adoring of the adored – true worship is loving Jesus, the lover of our souls.

---

90 Romans 5:4.
91 Ephesians 3:17–19 NIV.

Chapter 6

Everything in its Right Place

HONOURING THE HOLY IN WORSHIP

Neil Bennetts

God is generous beyond belief.

He pours out His blessing upon us.[92] He graces us with His presence.[93] He shares His thoughts and His desires with us.[94] He divulges His purpose and maps out plans that prosper us.[95] He brings us beauty out of ashes, and gives us garments of praise. He pours onto us His oil of gladness.[96]

He clothes us in His righteousness. He shines His light upon us. He invites us into a place of intimacy and sings tenderly to us.[97] He stands as a shield around us in times of testing.[98] He sets a banquet out before us and invites us to come and eat with Him.[99] He sent His only Son to die for us.[100] He sent His Spirit in power to breathe new life into us.[101]

He gives us every good and perfect gift.[102] He cares for us[103] and provides for us.[104]

---

92 Ephesians 1:3.
93 Psalm 16:11.
94 Proverbs 1:22.
95 Jeremiah 29:11.
96 Isaiah 61:3.
97 Zephaniah 3:17.
98 Psalm 3:3.
99 Matthew 22:4.
100 John 3:16.
101 John 6:63.
102 James 1:17.
103 1 Peter 5:7.
104 1 Timothy 6:17.

Yes, God is generous beyond belief.

But when it comes to His glory, God is jealous beyond belief. He won't share it with anyone.

Or, as the Message Bible puts it, He will not franchise it out.

"I am God. That's my name. I don't franchise my glory, don't endorse the no-god idols."[105]

When we worship, there is a very real sense that we are putting everything back into its rightful place. We are exalting God to the highest place so that He appears greater, and we appear less. We are placing His will and His ways above our own. We are aligning our hearts with His heart. Our minds with His mind. Our wills with His will. As we sing our songs in church, we are reminding ourselves of this correct order of things.

Then as we live our lives throughout the week, we allow those intentions expressed in song to permeate our whole lives as we serve our communities, do our jobs, spend time with our families. We are placing the honouring of God's ways and the magnification of His nature at the top of our agenda. We are purposely setting our eyes on the beautiful one, allowing the light of His presence to illuminate our ways and transform us into His likeness.

And in all of this, we are in every way possible saying, "God of Glory, have Your glory."[106]

Of course, we cannot add to God's greatness or His glory or His majesty with the words of our songs or the actions of our lives, because His greatness and His glory and His majesty are absolute and all-consuming. In fact, we kid ourselves if we ever think that anything we say, do, acknowledge or testify to makes God more God-like. His survival does not depend on our praise, our affirmations or our promises, because He is the one who was and is and is to come, regardless of our seemingly feeble refrains.

---

105 Isaiah 42:8 The Message.
106 I was inspired by this phrase, which comes from a song by Matt Redman and David Gate called "King of Glory".

But He does require us to honour who He is and what He does.

In fact, He loves it when we do.

He loves it when we put everything into its right place.

It pleases Him.

God of glory, have your glory.

A magnificent carnival of irreverent praise: When all is not well

As the ark is being taken back to Jerusalem,[107] we see an extraordinary celebration going on. David has chosen Jerusalem as the capital for the Israelites, and he is determined that the ark, this incredibly potent symbol not only of God's reality and God's reign for the Israelite people, but of His very presence with them, should be moved to Jerusalem as a part of setting that city aside for God.

Although the initial resting place for the ark in Jerusalem would be the tabernacle, the ark is destined for the Temple in Jerusalem that will ultimately be built under King Solomon's reign. The people of God will cease to be nomadic. They will have a spiritual home in Jerusalem, and they will have a permanent temple where God resides and which provides a focus for their worshipping life.

So this day was not a mere side-story for them − it was central to their journey as the people of God.

It was something that warranted a huge celebration.

It was a day that David had dreamed of for many years. From his very youngest days, David was concerned that God's rule and reign had become dishonoured amongst the people. The ark of the Lord had been hidden away, neglected for many years, and it was always David's dream to restore it to its rightful place.[108] He had longed for the ark, that was so often used merely as a mascot

107 2 Samuel 6:1–23.
108   Psalm 132:1–10.

in battle, to once again become central to worship. He longed for the ark, which was seemingly ignored during the reign of Saul, to be fully restored to its rightful place of prominence amongst the people of God. Such was his passion to establish a resting place for the ark that he determined to "allow no sleep to [his] eyes, no slumber to [his] eyelids" until it happened.[109]

Now, finally the day had arrived for David's dream to be fulfilled, and to celebrate it David organized this amazing carnival, this magnificent act of worship to mark the ark's journey to Jerusalem.

The whole nation was with him.[110]

David had conferred with his army. They had gathered the people. They had assembled the crowds and they had placed the ark on a new cart for transportation.[111]

You can really imagine the scene – a glorious fusion of dance, music and laughter, all mingled with a sense of triumphalism as a new age of prosperity beckoned for the people of God.

In fact, if we go back just a little more, this event follows a time of incredible success for David. He had been made king,[112] and had immediately gone to Jerusalem and made it his home.[113] He not only made the city bigger and stronger,[114] but also began to make his own position more powerful.[115] His family also grew in size, giving additional evidence as to the blessing of God on him. Then success with home and city and family was added to by success in battle against the Philistines, who were crushed by David and his army.[116]

Yes, David's star was in the ascendant. He was on a roll. The Lord God almighty was with him.[117] God's generosity abounded

---

109 Psalm 132:4.
110 2 Samuel 6:5.
111 1 Chronicles 13:5.
112 2 Samuel 5:4.
113 2 Samuel 5:9.
114 2 Samuel 5:9.
115 2 Samuel 5:10.
116 2 Samuel 5:25.
117 2 Samuel 5:10.

in him and around him, and amongst the people whom he ruled over. So this glorious procession carrying the ark to Jerusalem was fitting for both the king and the occasion.

But suddenly, totally against the grain, there is a stumble. The ark wobbles and looks set to topple over, and Uzzah, one of those trusted men that David has tasked with carrying the ark, reaches out a hand to try and stop it from falling.

This was a moment of madness.

As Uzzah puts out a hand, he grabs something he shouldn't and he is struck down.[118]

Dead.

In an instant.

We can all probably imagine the scene. One moment there is this colourful, joyous procession going on, a real high of energy and celebration. Then suddenly there is this instantaneous sense of horror, shock, loss, that came on them in that moment. In a second, the carnival atmosphere falls away, to be replaced by a tense, confused silence.

There is sense of disbelief, a sense of things totally being turned on their head in an instant. A sense of being robbed of something. A sense of disappointment. And as well as all of that, there is also probably a sense of total injustice because, let's face it, this probably does seem harsh. Uzzah's intention, after all, was almost certainly good – he was only trying to stop the ark from falling.

It would be very easy to argue that he was only doing his job.

Yet there he was, lying dead on the ground in the dirt.

Maybe this is why David's first reaction is to get angry.[119]

In one sense, who can blame him? The aim of the journey was correct – to restore the ark to its central place. The purpose of the procession was a worthy one – to celebrate the generosity of God and make his praise glorious. Even Uzzah was arguably acting in a reasonable manner and with the best of intentions –

---

118 2 Samuel 6:7.
119 2 Samuel 6:8.

to stop the ark from falling. You can almost hear David's cries:

"We did all of this for you, God! We put all of this on for you. This was the result of a dream you placed in my heart many years ago.

"Can't you see how much effort we've put in? We've sacrificed so much time, money and effort to make it all happen. We thought you were with us.

"And now... this!"

However, very quickly David seems to realize what has happened. He suddenly becomes aware that everything was not in its right place, and that this act was irreverent: both he and Uzzah should have known that the touching of holy things led to death.[120]

So very quickly, David's anger gives way to a holy fear.[121]

As David realizes the irreverence of Uzzah's actions, and the resulting display of God's wrath and anger against him, he learns something.

He learns that when we touch on the generosity of God, we touch on His holiness.

He won't express His generosity in ways that will compromise who He is.

In fact, it's not only that He won't, He can't.

I wonder if this was one of those "reality check" moments for David. After a season of everything going so well – his success in everything he touched – he was reminded of the source and reason for that success. The source of the success was God, and the reason for the success was the glory of God.

One could even imagine how those recent victories had caused David to become just a little bit conceited, maybe a little full of himself. I don't know. It is certainly not obvious from the text. All I can say is that if this was me, I would have struggled to keep things in perspective. There is always the danger, with a successful ministry, of slipping into ways of doing things that

120 Numbers 4:15.
121   2 Samuel 6:9.

make it seem like some of what is happening is for us. A little bit here, a little bit there. We may even talk ourselves around to thinking that we have to "bear a little of the limelight for ourselves" in order that God receives the higher glory.

But actually, God's holiness demands that it's all for Him.

The songs we write, the ministries we run, the programmes we put on – it's all for Him. There is no state we should embrace that allows us to receive any glory for what we do. It is all for Him. Every pound and penny, every mention in the press, every favourable review, every inch gained in the Kingdom of God. It's all for Him.

God of glory, have your glory.

A reality check: Taking stock of where we are

I have been extremely fortunate to have been part of Trinity Cheltenham over the years – a church that has grown in both numbers and in reach in terms of its ministry. My friendship and working partnership with Mark Bailey, our lead pastor, over the years has been amazing. I have also had the incredible joy of being part of the New Wine movement during that time, leading worship at many of its events and conferences and contributing to many of its worship recordings.

My involvement with both my church and the New Wine movement has meant that I have become more involved in the UK worship scene and beyond – far more than I ever expected to – and have had the chance to work with some of the most anointed and gifted worship leaders from around the world. It has been an incredible journey – one that I anticipate continuing on for many years to come.

Naturally, alongside all of this there have been things I have come across in the whole arena of church worship that I have struggled with – and still do. I have also had cause to regret some of my own decisions along the way. So as I've read this account of Uzzah again in recent months, I have found myself re-examining what I have been involved with in the whole area of worship – both as a worship leader and as one of the pastors of a large church – and also reassessing what I see the wider church dealing with. I have needed to experience some sort of reality check of my own.

And I guess the overriding question I keep asking myself is this: is God really getting the glory He is due?

Is what I am doing, we are doing, the church is doing, really for God's glory alone or am I, we, my church, my network, engaged – in any sense – in our own carnival of irreverent praise? Am I engaged in something that, on the face of it, looks exciting, attractive, colourful, and creative, but something that at its heart has something irreverent – something that started out as a fresh, vibrant expression of the Spirit's creativity, but has ended up in something that is carnal, full of the flesh, full of me?

It's a good question to ask, because I don't want me, my church, or anyone else, for that matter, to end up lying dead on the floor in the dirt. You see, whereas I am sure that God loves the creativity and colour in the things I do in worship, and surely delights in them, I am pretty convinced that they do not blind Him. He can surely see right through them into my heart and know whether I do them out of reverence before Him or because of attention-seeking for me.

So as I have done this reality check for myself, there have been a few areas that I have been challenged with:

The unsexy path of biblical orthodoxy: Keeping worship true to Scripture

I can't explain why in this instance, Uzzah's disobedience led to his almost instantaneous death. Such occurrences are thankfully few and far between in the Bible – although it certainly isn't one of those "Old Testament only" things, because something very similar happens to Ananias and Sapphira in Acts 5:5, this time because they were not entirely open and up-front on some financial issues. Whether or not we can quite get our heads round the severity of the judgment of God on Uzzah, what happened on that day was the result of two mistakes – both of which had their roots in a lack of adherence to the word of God.

The first we have touched on – that Uzzah was in breach of God's written law when He touched the ark – but if we rewind a little bit we discover more about this event and probably the root cause. When David had prepared for this day, we read that he had consulted his officers, and consulted his people, and they had all agreed that bringing the ark back was a good thing to do.[122] But it seems that along the way, David's enthusiasm had caused him to forget something.

He had forgotten to seek out the opinion of God.

He had forgotten to seek the voice of the Lord.[123] He had sought out the opinion of the many, but had not sought out the opinion of The One. If he had sought out God, he would have probably remembered that the ark shouldn't have been put on a new cart, it should have been held high on poles on the shoulder of the Levites, "as Moses had commanded in accordance with the word of the Lord."[124]

So as they set out on that journey, everything was clearly not in its right place.

There was no doubt that David had set himself and his men to the task in hand with great enthusiasm. There is no doubt that his heart was after the Lord. There is no doubt that his actions were rooted in absolutely top-hole A-1 intentions, but in his absence to inquire properly of the Lord before he set out, everything was not put in its right place. God's instructions were clear but they had not been pursued, let alone taken to heart

---

122 1 Chronicles 13:1–4.
123 1 Chronicles 15:13.
124 1 Chronicles 15:15.

by David. To coin a well-worn but profound phrase: David may have gone a good way, but he did not go the God way.

Being biblical, or theological, or sound is not particularly sexy these days when we talk about worship. We prefer words such as powerful, poetic, creative, innovative, or fresh. The trouble is that unless it is biblical, worship is irreverent, and all these other things become meaningless or even destructive. Whether it's in the presentation of our music, or in the content of our songs lyrics, or in the construction of our worship services, we have to be profoundly biblical.

I hear many people expressing a desire for many things in worship, but I don't often hear people saying that they want to experience more truth – more truth about God, and more truth about who He really is and what He really thinks. Yet it is truth that sets us free. So let's not get caught up in things in worship that are not biblical, however exciting, creative, fresh, or even seemingly fruitful and popular, because ultimately they will collapse around us.

The refining power of a holy God: God will protect His reputation

As we have seen, the ark was the most potent symbol of God's presence for the Israelites, and when God's presence is greatest, we should expect to experience more of His holiness.

Many of us will testify to the fact that as we grow closer to God on our journey of discipleship, we tend to become more aware of our weakness and sinfulness, not less aware, so this isn't a totally alien concept for us. One of the descriptions of God's presence in the Bible is as a consuming fire,[125] and so if the sense of God's presence is greater, then maybe we should expect God's refining process to be more powerful and evident. Isn't this what happened to Isaiah when he was commissioned in Isaiah 6 – an amazing encounter with God, followed by the

---

125 Deuteronomy 4:24.

refining activity of His holiness?[126]

If your church is like our church, you are constantly crying out to the Lord for Him to show us more of His presence. I wonder if you, like me, are more inclined to see that evidenced in a display of generosity rather than the activity of refinement?

I recently heard Rich Nathan, a vineyard pastor in the USA,[127] say that he had read that when God's outpourings are at their highest and when the manifestation of His presence is greatest, if people are casual in worship, if they continue to sin in such circumstances of revival, more of them actually get sick or even die. Now I don't know how much substantive evidence there is on this, or even if you could ever actually statistically prove it, but I wouldn't be surprised if it was true.

This is probably one of the things that most scares me most about being a worship leader. God's presence inhabits the praises of His people, so when we gather to worship we should expect to experience a greater measure of His refining holiness – and here is me trying to lead it. It's exciting and worrying all at the same time. It makes me altogether more humble, and more careful than maybe I otherwise would be.

The powerless torso of a broken idol: The danger of making worship an idol

Looking further back into the history of Israel, we see another sequence of events surrounding the ark. This time we see the ark being captured from Israel by the Philistines.[128] The Philistines take the ark, the spoils of their battles with the people of God, to a seaport called Ashdod, and place it in the temple of Dagon,[129] one of their own no-god idols. We read how the next day the Philistines return to find Dagon face down before the ark. The Philistines put Dagon back in his place, but when they return

---

126 Isaiah 6:8.
127 Sermon, "The Integrity-Filled Church", Vineyard Columbus, 22 August 2010.
128 1 Samuel 4:11.
129 1 Samuel 5:2.

the next day, again they not only find Dagon has fallen down, but that he has broken into pieces:

> the following morning when they rose, there was
> Dagon, fallen on his face on the ground before the
> ark of the Lord! His head and hands had been broken
> off and were lying on the threshold; only his body
> remained.[130]

Here was Dagon, most probably a fish-god who was worshipped as a way of attempting to ensure provision of food, face down and broken before the ark of God. His head and hands had been broken off, making him unable to see, smell, hear or do anything. He was unable to sense anything, or perform any deeds whatsoever. He was completely broken before God.

There are echoes of this moment in Psalm 115:

> Where is their God? Our God is in heaven! He does
> whatever He pleases! Their idols are made of silver
> or gold – they are man-made. They have mouths but
> cannot speak, eyes but cannot see, ears but cannot
> hear, noses but cannot smell, hands but cannot touch,
> feet, but cannot walk. They cannot even clear their
> throats.[131]

Of course, this act by the Philistines was a much more blatant dishonouring of God than Uzzah's – very probably they had put the ark in the temple of Dagon in a purposeful attempt to humiliate God – but it seems to me that anyone or anything that attempts to compete with the glory of God will ultimately fail.

Even worship itself.

It is entirely possible for us to make worship itself an idol, to honour the process of worship above the object of our worship. We do it when we get precious about things that we shouldn't

---

130 1 Samuel 5:4.
131 Psalm 115:2–7 NET.

get precious about. We do it when we get our own identities too entwined in our ministries. We do it when we hold onto things tightly as if they are things we own rather than things entrusted to us. We do it when we label things as "sacred" in order to protect our own self-interest in them. We even start to do it when we go to church on a Sunday and become a consumer of worship – demanding our preferences and being critical of what is being served up to us.

Worship is special. It is something incredibly treasured and close to the heart of God, and it seems to me that those of us who are involved in worship in any way need to be aware of this. Worship is special, and we need to be almost more careful with it than with anything else.

People deal with these things in different ways. The way I have tried to deal with it is by purposefully removing myself from things that could potentially cause me to make an idol out of worship.

Maybe I have missed out on some things because of that. I don't really know. Actually I don't count myself as particularly brilliant at what I do. In fact I sometimes wonder whether, compared with the skill and creativity of most other worship leaders and musicians, God has blessed me with an averageness that has kept me particularly dependent on Him. But even so, maybe I could be doing more things in the whole worship scene, recording more albums, leading worship at bigger events, writing songs that are being used in more churches around the world. Maybe I could, and maybe it's because I know that the temptations could have been too much for me to deal with well that I have not tried to go this way. But I made the decision many years ago that I would distance myself from anything that, for me, could make the process of worship more important than the person I worship.

I've found that it is all too easy to hide behind my good intentions when to stand openly and honesty in the brightness of God's holiness would leave me seriously wanting.

I can't answer for people who tour and do worship concerts. I can't answer for those worship leaders who purposefully try to serve the church by getting their songs sung in more and more countries around the world. I can't answer for those worship leaders who stand up in front of other worship leaders and receive awards for their songs. I really can't answer for them. However, I can answer for myself, and I know that for me, the dangers of making worship an idol are too great, and so I have purposefully avoided such things, because I know that, like any idol in this life, my own worship idol could come crashing down overnight.

Face down.

Broken.

Because God doesn't share His glory.

The subtle whisper of intoxicating fame: Reflecting praise back on to God

I remember reading a newspaper interview in 2010 with one of the world's most famous and high-profile footballers who was nearing retirement. He was recounting the highlights of his career, and as he did so it was interesting to see that the moments that he counted amongst his most memorable were not those where he had displayed the most skill, but those moments where the adulation of the crowd had been at its greatest. This particular footballer, in my mind, dealt well with his profile but I am sure that we can all think of many such sportsmen, film stars, and celebrities who haven't dealt with it very well, who have blown up in the process. People whose hearts have been tested by fame, and have been found wanting.

Equally we can also probably think of many high-profile worship leaders or church leaders who have also not dealt with it well, and ended up losing their ministry. I am sure there are many reasons for such things, but I wonder if one of them is because they didn't learn how to deal well with the praise or profile they received?

Proverbs says: "The purity of human hearts is tested by giving them a little fame."[132]

When praise or profile or recognition comes our way, it tests us, and it seems to me that one sure way of dealing with praise or recognition badly is to feed off it. To start to believe in it too much. To start to build our lives and ministries around getting more of it. This sort of attitude is dangerous because the praise we receive for what we do can be intoxicating.

Like a drug, it can consume us.

OK, so this sounds good, but actually what does it mean in practice? After all, we can't stop people congratulating us for what we do. We can't stop people writing good reviews about our ministry, our leadership, our songs or our sermons.

Of course we can't.

What we can do, though, is make sure we don't go out of our way to court profile or recognition in an unhealthy way. I have decided that this means focusing on what I am called to do: write songs for my church, lead worship for my church in the most God-honouring way that I can, and be as obedient to His call on my life day by day as I can possibly be. Anything else, I leave up to God to sort out. If He wants a song to travel the world, I think He is able to do it without undue pressure from me. If He wants me to reach places of greater influence and responsibility in my ministry, then He is able to make the pathway clear.

In fact I wonder whether we would generally have more great churches in the UK if we had less great ministries? I wonder whether if we were really more passionate about the success of our churches, and less concerned about the success of our ministries, then we would see the Kingdom growing faster than it is at the moment?

I heard Tim Keller recently talking about mission. He said that he had come to realize that most people think about using

132 Proverbs 27:21 (The Message).

their town to build a great church, when actually they should think about using their church to build a great town. I wonder – to use the same sort of language – whether too many of us use our churches to build a great ministry, rather than use our ministry to build a great church.

The model of Jesus is one of someone who gave things up, who chose the path of humility, who made Himself nothing. Paul, too, urges us to do nothing out of selfish ambition or vain conceit.[133] Not a little, not a few bits here and there, but nothing.

Zero.

Zilch.

Despite what the famous strapline says, my view is this: just don't do it if it is in any way motivated by the desire to promote self or to feed insecurity.

As Paul goes on to express, it was God who raised Jesus up. God was the one who exalted Him to the highest place.[134] The part that Jesus played was to be obedient, and humble, and self-effacing. This is the path we should tread too. If there is any exalting to be done, let us allow God Himself to do it.

A little while back I received a marketing email about a particular worship leader that encouraged me to buy his worship album for a number of reasons, one of which was because this worship leader had been voted "one of the country's most beautiful people" in some survey. Now maybe I'm just a little bit too sensitive to such things, but it just made me feel so disappointed. I'm all for people wanting to be and do beautiful things in the Kingdom, but in my view, someone who is beautiful in the Kingdom of God is someone who purposely defers any limelight to God, not someone who purposely goes out of their way to draw attention to themselves.

A truly beautiful life, in fact, may never purposely seek the adulation of the world, but probably has learned how to deal

133 Philippians 2:3.
134 Philippians 2:9.

with it when it comes. A beautiful life lived for the glory of God may from time to time attract the attention of a curious world, but very quickly all eyes defer to the Creator behind the created, the one who is true beauty itself.

Every time I see an advert like the one I mentioned, every time I see a worship concert tour being unhealthily advertised, every time I see someone's website that indicates an obsession with a person's own ministry, every time I see these things I sense that people's eyes are being drawn away from God and I wonder whether we are slowly inching their hands out, trying to grab some glory for ourselves.

Of course, for most of us, the testing is far more subtle, far quieter than a press report or a marketing circular. For most of us it is that faint whisper that we hear when we least expect it – that faint whisper of praise that promises a little bit more recognition, a little more wealth, a little more profile. And here is what I've found – that the only way to deal with it is to pass it on to God. Reflect any praise or glory or recognition back to Him. The praise we receive will be safer resting with Him than burrowing its way into our own hearts where it could do no end of damage.

Holding on lightly to the non-sacred sacred: Letting go of the sacred cow

I remember from many years back when I was involved in a new venture at a church I was part of. We tried to move our worship gently on by having a couple of sung items at the start of the evening service while people were still coming in and getting settled. The first time we did it, we had one hymn on the organ followed by one "worship song" from the music group. It went quite well, I seem to remember. The next time as we planned the service, someone suggested that instead of one hymn and one "worship song" we should have two "worship songs". Immediately someone piped up in protest that we should have one hymn and one song because "We've always done it that way."

We had only done it once! Yet it had, at least in this person's mind, become a tradition.

It's amazing how soon we latch on to something and give it a standing in history or a sacredness in worship that it just doesn't deserve. We all too easily make the non-sacred sacred.

This current generation of worship leaders, of which I am part, has been handed an incredibly important and significant responsibility in the history of the church. We are in many ways like those people in David's procession, carrying the presence of God through and amongst the people of God. God has entrusted us with a holy task, not only to carry it with care in our generation, but to safely transfer it on to the next, and we need to carefully examine ourselves as to whether we are doing this as well as we can.

Many years ago, when our churches were full and Britain was a Christian nation, our worship was led by a generation of extremely gifted, committed, and wonderful organists and their choirs. Those times are not that long ago. In the seventies, when I was growing up, worship at church still meant singing the hymns of Wesley, accompanied by the organ and a choir. It was – and still is – awesome music, and released incredible praise amongst the people of God. Such expressions of praise are far more rare these days.

Then as culture changed, and as different expressions of creativity grew within the church over the seventies and eighties, rather than it bringing colour and new life to the church, a battleground was formed between the organists and worship leaders. Gradually, the issue that became dominant was not the release of praise amongst the people of God, but the protection of musical style in the church. I was myself caught up in this battleground, and was probably as much to blame as anyone else for some of the disunity that arose.

As I reflect on these times, many years later, I wonder whether the desire to hold on to this traditional musical style and call it "sacred" was the very cause of its downfall. Maybe, just maybe, the musical style and process became too important, and started to become an idol itself? Of course, I can understand this in some ways – traditional church music had been such a hugely influential part of the life of the church and Kingdom activity, and the churches had been full. So I can understand the reluctance of many people to let such things go.

However, whereas I am very interested in the events and motivations of people in the past, I am actually more concerned about my own motivations in this season. The challenge to me is to make sure I don't go the same way, that I don't make my music, and my worship style, the sacred thing, when there is no biblical justification for calling it sacred at all. C. S. Lewis said this:

> There are two musical situations on which I think I can be confident that a blessing rests. One is where a priest or organist, himself a man of trained and delicate taste, humbly and charitably sacrifices his own (aesthetically right) desires and gives the people humbler and coarser fare than he would wish, in a belief that he can thus bring them to God. The other is where the stupid and unmusical layman humbly and patiently, and above all silently, listens to music which he cannot, or cannot fully, appreciate, in the belief that it somehow glorifies God, and that if it does not edify him this must be his own defect. But where the musician is filled with the pride or skill or the virus of emulation and looks with contempt on the unappreciative congregation, or where the unmusical, complacently entrenched in their own ignorance and conservatism, look with restless and resentful hostility of an inferior complex on all who would try to improve

their taste – there, we may be sure, all that both offer is unblessed and the spirit that moves them is not the Holy Ghost.[135]

I was strangely challenged a while ago when I realized that not only was I dispensable as a worship leader, but what I was embodying in my style of worship was also totally dispensable. Somehow along the way I had begun to believe that what I was doing was somehow untouchable. The middle-of-the-road, Radio 2, soft-rock, evangelical, charismatic, easy-going worship style that I was doing – and still am – was somehow the way it should be for ever more. Amen. I came to realize that what I had been thinking of as sacred was not sacred at all. It was the non-sacred sacred. Something I was giving a sense of eternal value that had no biblical grounding at all. The recent worship movement of which I have been a part for the last twenty-five years could disappear in an instant and be replaced.

So who gets the glory? Who is honoured by what we do, when we do it?

A recent three-year survey undertaken by Gallop asked 3,000 Americans what they most required from their political, community, educational, or church leaders. The most important quality was trust – followed by compassion, stability, and hope. Above everything else, people wanted to be able to trust their leaders. Integrity was the prime quality that Americans wanted from their leaders. Not fruitfulness. Not the ability to generate wealth. Not the ability to provide services. Not the ability to educate them to the highest possible standard.

Integrity.

Trust.

I would resonate with this opinion. I would say the most important characteristic I would look for in a leader would be

---

135 Taken from an essay entitled "On Church Music".

integrity. In fact I would prefer to know the truth even if the truth was not to my best advantage.

So maybe I shouldn't be surprised if His integrity is the quality that God will not allow to be compromised under any circumstances. In fact God is ultimately concerned with His glory above all else because it is impossible for Him to allow His integrity, His character, His holiness to be undermined. Maybe that's why God will always let seemingly very fruitful things wither and die if they start to undermine His integrity.

So let me ask you this. When you stand up to sing on a Sunday morning – who gets the glory?

When the Spirit of God dwells more powerfully in your church as you lead, or speak, or pray – who gets the glory?

When the ministry you are involved with starts to fly and make a huge impact in your church, town, or beyond – who gets the glory?

When you write a new song and sing it in church – who gets the glory?

When you record a worship album that gets favourable reviews in the press – who gets the glory?

When you plan your diary and accept invitations and travel – who gets the glory?

When you do the new thing, the creative thing, that clever thing with your voice, your guitar, your band – who gets the glory?

Not "Who do you want to get the glory?" or "Who do you intend will get the glory?" or "Who gets the most glory?" – but who actually gets the glory?

All of it.

God?

I am not the sort of person who loves those expressions we use, such as "make me nothing" or "less of me". In fact when I was involved in a more traditional Anglican set-up, we used to say a prayer as part of the communion service that had the line,

"We are not worthy so much as to gather up the crumbs from under your table." I found that just a little hard to get my head around. We used to call it the "humble crumble prayer". I didn't particularly like it because my understanding is that God wants me, not so much to become nothing, but to become everything He intended – life in all its fullness and adventure and effectiveness in the Kingdom. I want to become the sort of leader who enters into the fullness of everything God has prepared for me.

But it just seems that I can use what He gives me or makes me to draw attention either to Him, or to me.

Everything in its right place

Let us return to David who, if we remember, has just had this terrifying wake-up call with the death of Uzzah. Whatever David's attitude leading up to this event, his attitude after it was clear.

He was shaking in his boots.[136]

The power of God that had shown no bounds in generosity was now showing no compromise in holiness and suddenly having the ark, having the presence of God so evident and close to him in Jerusalem was not looking like such an attractive prospect. So he instead decided to hide it away in the house of Obed-Edom rather than take it to Jerusalem.[137] A bit of breathing space, maybe. A little time to process what had happened. A time of reflection and listening to God for some explanations, possibly.

We are not told how Obed-Edom initially reacted to that. My guess is that he wasn't too chuffed with the idea. This ark, which had just caused the instantaneous death of someone who, on the face of it, didn't really seem to do much to justify his demise, was now thrust upon his household.

One can only imagine the trepidation as the course of the

136 2 Samuel 6:9.
137 2 Samuel 6:10.

ark's journey is changed and it ends up in Obed's front room, but we must assume that he treated it with the respect it deserved, because he and his whole household were blessed.

One of the psalms that David wrote maybe hints at what David learnt this day. The psalm says that those who experience the most amazing generosity of God – His nearness, His closeness, His friendship – are those who have come to understood exactly who He is – His holiness, His majesty, His greatness.

His friendship is reserved for those who fear Him.[138]

He won't express His generosity in ways that compromise who He is.

At the end of this episode we find David armed with his new-found understanding, going back for the ark, to once again try to bring it to Jerusalem. Once again a carnival is arranged. Only this time, there is a significant change.

There are still the musicians, there is still the music and the dance. Only this time there is something else. Firstly, the ark is carried in the right way[139] and secondly, the heady proceedings are interspersed with regular stops to make animal sacrifices to God. This time the sights and sounds and the colours are mingled with the smell of burnt animal flesh.

Two animals – a bull and a calf – are given up to God every six steps.

Every few steps, David is building in a checkpoint. He is building in a moment to double-check that things are still on course, that things are still being done as they should be.

Every six steps he is just reminding himself of the lines of holiness that are drawn in the sand.

Every six steps he is holding up all that is happening to very visibly make every possible effort to ensure that he, or anyone under his care, is not in danger of putting out a hand and taking glory away from God.

This time, things go a little more smoothly.

---

138 Psalm 25:14.
139 1 Chronicles 15:15.

More slowly, yes, but much more smoothly.

And the ark finishes its journey to Jerusalem and is placed in the tabernacle. As we know, it will ultimately rest in the Temple, but that is still a little way off.

But it does come to rest in Jerusalem.

And David himself finds rest for a season.

David's desire to take the ark to Jerusalem probably echoes our own desires to know and experience the presence of God in our lives, and when we worship together, more than ever we long for such times to be typified by the manifest presence of God – a real sense of Him being actually with us in a real and tangible and active way.

As part of this we should be people who long to know and celebrate His incredible generosity. We are people who sing songs about God being all we need, being our portion, being our strength, and we are all humbled when that evidences itself in our lives.

But as we set our eyes on His generosity, let us not shield our eyes to the brightness of His holiness.

Let us have a passion to celebrate His generosity and an equal passion to honour His holiness in all that we seek to do.

God of glory, have your glory.

Chapter 7

Coram Deo – Living Life to the Face of God

THE PRESENCE AND POWER OF GOD IN WORSHIP

Neil Bennetts

When people worship God passionately and authentically in the Bible, they experience His presence and build a platform for Him to move in power.

In the place of passionate and authentic worship we experience the manifest presence of God.[140] As we draw near in worship to Him, He draws near to us.[141] As we sing our praises to Him, He, in a very real and active way, inhabits those praises.[142] And as we experience the manifest presence of God, we experience the power of God, which brings about His Kingdom activity. So in the place of worship, prison walls come falling down,[143] the enemies of God are destroyed,[144] the broken-hearted find their strength,[145] the unbelievers are drawn into the Kingdom,[146] we see people transformed into the likeness of God,[147] we see people become totally satisfied as children of the King,[148] and we see

---

140 2 Chronicles 7:1.
141 James 4:8.
142 Psalm 22:3.
143 Acts 16:26.
144 2 Chronicles 20:22.
145 Psalm 73:26.
146 1 Corinthians 14:25.
147 2 Corinthians 3:18.
148 Psalm 63:5.

people compelled to pursue a journey of radical discipleship.[149]

This Kingdom activity that happens when we worship can be a small voice of comfort heard by a broken heart, it can be a mighty wind blowing though a barren land, it can be the uncontrollable sobbing of a repentant soul, it can be the irreversible healing of a damaged limb, it can be the peaceful settling of a long-held fear, it can be the painful realignment of a rebellious nature to the will of God. This Kingdom activity is not always immediately noticeable or heralded by the dramatic. It can be silent and tender and gentle as much as it can be explosive. It can be a seismic shift in character or physical state, or a single tentative step towards the Father. But whatever nature it takes, it is powerful. Deep has called to deep. The heart of man has been touched by the heart of God, and it will never be the same.

Of course, God is not limited in the way He moves by the intensity of our worship. He managed to reveal Himself to Saul with blinding light without a single line being sung.[150] He managed to part the Red Sea without the accompaniment of a melody,[151] and He managed to create the heavens and the earth before we even existed, let alone found our voice.[152] We should never forget this. He is the great "I am". He is, and has, the Name that is above every name, and ultimately there is nothing good that happens in heaven or on earth that is not initiated by His grace, motivated by His generosity, crafted by His mercy and fulfilled through His good and perfect faithfulness.[153]

But somewhere within the mystery that is the Kingdom of God, we are invited to join in with His purposes and activity. We are invited to sing songs and speak words and perform deeds that usher in His presence, that herald acts of His grace and power. Somewhere in the mystery that is the Kingdom of God, He asks us to draw alongside Him and be very much part of bringing His

---

149 Isaiah 6:8.
150 Acts 9:3.
151 Exodus 14:21.
152 Genesis 1.
153 James 1:17.

light into the darkness around us.

It is an invitation not from a limited God who is somehow restrained from acting out His sovereignty, but from a jealous God who is courting the affection of His world, who is actively seeking out worship from us.[154] It is an invitation from a generous God who wants us to know His strength and His transforming power at work in our lives, and travel the journey of the Kingdom in partnership with Him.

Because of our "Yes": Worship that builds a platform for God

I remember once going to someone's wedding, many years ago, and during the signing of the register someone played a great musical work on a very fine grand piano in the church. The piece was played with consummate accuracy. It was note perfect. The piano itself was incredible, full of rich, perfect tones, with no creaking pedals. But the piece as it was played that day was devoid of emotion. It was empty. The piece as it was played was technically brilliant but lacked anything that brought it truly alive. The moment didn't come close to touching my heart.

In fact I would probably go as far as to say I was upset. I went away feeling that it would have been better had the piece not been played at all, that it would have been better to have sat through the signing of the register in silence.

You see, if our worship of God stops with the well-crafted songs that we sing, with the beautiful sounds that our bands make, with the precious artefacts that adorn our buildings or with the creative excellence of our visual presentations, it is empty. Devoid of meaning. Irrelevant. In fact it can even become an insult to God Himself.[155] If we take Kingdom activity out of worship we are just firing blanks. We may get a lot of noise and smoke and fireworks and draw a measure of attention from those

154 John 4.
155 Amos 5:22.

around us, but we will have no power.

We may as well stay silent.

There is a thread that wraps itself around every act of singing, every act of adoration, every Sunday morning programme, that brings worship its authenticity, that causes our words and our tunes and our harmonies to echo in the Kingdom of God. There is a thread that wraps itself around our efforts, our desires, our activity, our pursuit of excellence, our creative endeavours and causes them to please God.

And that thread is the thread of obedience.

If, like me, you often echo the words of the Lord's prayer[156] and cry "Your Kingdom come", then we have to accept that this will involve more than a few carefully chosen words, however well thought out and crafted, because our obedience and the advancement of the Kingdom are inextricably linked. When we are obedient to the voice of God, when we are living out the "Your will be done" as His people, then we are engaging with His presence, engaging with His power in us, engaging with His Kingdom purposes on earth.

So as I reflect on the place of worship in our churches, I believe that if we want to see more Kingdom activity as we sing, then it won't first and foremost be because of our great songs, our clever band arrangements, our well-produced CDs, or our beautifully constructed song sets, however important those things are.

It will be because of our "Yes".

Because of our "Yes".

It is when we are obedient, doing the things He is doing, seeing the things that He is seeing, walking the road that He is walking, singing the things that He is singing, that will see His Kingdom break through in our lives and into the people and situations around us. When we allow the touch of God's heart to cause us to respond in glad surrender to His ways, then we welcome His rule and His reign into our lives and situations,

---

156 Matthew 6:9–13.

and He is given permission to move.

As Jack Hayford put it: "His dealings with humankind are flavoured by a self-imposed insistence that He await the welcome of human hearts who consciously decide they want Him in their lives."[157]

The language of obedience

The world struggles with the language of obedience.

If we're honest, the church probably does as well.

The word speaks of oppression and the removal of rights and self-determination. When the word "obedience" is used, our first reaction is to think of how a dog responds to its owner, how a slave responds to his master, or how a subservient employee responds to a controlling and overbearing boss. However, when the Bible uses the language of obedience, it is normally used in a very different context: it is used in the context of loving relationship.

When Jesus asks us to be obedient, He does it in the understanding that we are in a loving relationship with Him, that we abide in Him. As He said: "As the Father has loved me, so have I loved you. Now remain in my love. If you obey my commands, you will remain in my love, just as I have obeyed my Father's commands and remain in his love."[158]

Our obedience is based on our relationship with Him above everything else, and our relationship with God is a covenant relationship – one where we choose to place ourselves under His rule and reign in our lives – a choice that flows out of the revelation, experience and understanding of His grace.

Jesus Himself lived a life of obedience, rooted in His relationship with the Father. He lived His life seeing what the Father was doing and going with it. Every act of mercy, every demonstration of power, every touch of grace was a response of

---

157 *Manifest Presence*, Sovereign Word, 2005, p. 25.
158 John 15:9–10.

obedience to God. Even His death was itself an act of obedience.[159] But even though Jesus went to that death willingly, it was not as though He didn't have choices, the ability to escape from His eternal purpose. The garden of Gethsemane is (according to most historians) on the edge of Jerusalem, at the foot of the Mount of Olives. In Jesus' day it would have been a great place from which to initiate an escape.

Apparently, if you went away from Jerusalem over the Mount of Olives in those days, you would have had access to many roads that would have taken you to various cities and towns where you would have been able to hide. It was a strategic place where Jesus would have had the option to flee from, if He had so chosen. In fact, David, many years earlier, had escaped from Absalom by fleeing from Jerusalem over the Mount of Olives, towards a small village called Bahurim.[160] So it is probably not to hard to imagine that as Jesus pleaded with His Father, in the garden of Gethsemane at the foot of the Mount, for the cup to "be taken from him"[161] that awaited Him, very much in His mind would have been the fact that around Him were many roads He could have taken to literally escape His destiny.

Jesus, though fully God, was also fully man, and in that moment He, in every way possible, had a choice before Him: to be obedient or not.

That's the thing about obedience in the Kingdom of God: it always involves choice, and it always involves choice because it is based on a relationship. I sometimes wonder how much easier life would be if God asked us to live by formula based on rules rather than faith based on relationship, but of course it would have no sense of adventure, no authenticity if it was. And let's face it, who really wants to live like that?

---

159 Philippians 2:8.
160 2 Samuel 15.
161 Matthew 26:39.

The choice of loving God

The call that God makes to all of us is this: "Will you love me? Will you worship me?"

Have you noticed that Jesus never insisted people love Him? He urged them to love Him, He revealed His goodness and power in such a way that many people were compelled to love Him, but He never insisted. As He walked the earth the created elements – wind, seas, sun – they all came under His command. Death, sickness, the powers of evil – they all came under His command. But to men and women everywhere, He only offered – and still offers – a choice: to love God, to worship God, or not.

At some point, we all have to make that choice for ourselves, and for Jesus, this choice to love God is a choice to love Him with everything. As Jesus summarized the commandments, He urged us all to love God – to love God with all our heart, mind, soul, and strength.[162]

It is a testing call, isn't it? To love God with everything. It seems that we will never be able to fulfil it. It seems that Jesus puts a call in front of us that we are inevitably going to fail. However, just as much as these words of Jesus are a command to us, they are also an expression of the value God puts on our affection. By placing this command at the top of the list, Jesus is not only us calling us to live lives of devotion to God, but He is sharing with us what the Father most of all wants from us.

Our hearts.

Our love.

Our devotion.

Before anything else.

I don't know about you, but I look around our gatherings of worship sometimes and question whether we are really, really worshipping with as much passion and conviction as we could be. I know I am making a really sweeping statement here – and I know there are many great exceptions. However, I do think

162 Matthew 22:37.

that generally, in the early part of the second decade in the third millennium AD, the church, particularly in the West, seems to have lost a little of its capacity and desire to love God. To show Him affection. To show Him devotion. One of my friends is the worship leader Jules Woodbridge, and she says it is like in the story of Jesus being anointed at Bethany (which is looked at in more detail in chapter three), where so many people wanted to discuss and debate and socialize, but in doing so had forgotten that Jesus was actually present and had feet that needed attention.

It's as though the church has lost sight of its first call – to be lovers of Him.

I truly believe that if we could only recapture this, then we would know the smile of God, the presence of God, the activity of God more powerfully.

What do you hear when you cannot hear? Worship that goes beyond the music

At New Wine recently one of the worship leaders who was working with me was approached by two men who started to engage in conversation with him. It soon became apparent that one of the men was deaf, and had difficulty speaking. The other man was clearly his mouthpiece in the conversation, and as they spoke it also became apparent that the deaf man was also not a Christian but had been brought along to New Wine by his friend.

Through a mixture of hand signals and translated words, this man said that although he couldn't hear the worship, and although he didn't know Jesus, he could feel the worship in his heart.

This man was deaf, and he wasn't even a Christian, but he felt the worship!

As the thousands of people in that celebration that evening intentionally and passionately sang their songs, God moved amongst us and worked His Kingdom purposes. His presence touched the heart of a man who didn't know Him, who probably was there under duress, and who couldn't even hear the sound of the band or the sound of the voices around him.

Don't you see how worship has to go far beyond the music? Or as David Ruis puts it: "What do we hear when we cannot hear?"

Well, for me, it is this: what is actually happening when we sing that marks us out from other groups, choirs, crowds, and concerts? It is that through our obedient response to God in worship, we are touched by the very heart of God as we sing.

As we sing, God sings.

As we love on Him, He loves on us.

Following in the footsteps of the Father: Costly choices in worship

As a leadership team recently, we had a day of prayer and fasting. We were spending time thinking through our vision for the next season in the life of our church, and mid morning we all found ourselves flat on the floor on our faces in the middle of the church building. I sensed God speak to me in that moment and say this: "You can hear my footsteps more clearly down here."

I was reminded again of the story of King Jehoshaphat in 2 Chronicles. Jehoshaphat was one of the kings of Judah. He was, in my mind, one of the better kings – although, of course, the competition was not great. He was, like King David before him, a man whose heart was devoted to the ways of the Lord. He was, like David before him, formidable in battle, in relationships, in influence, in love. But he, like David, also made some big mistakes – such as going to war with Ahab (a worshipper of Baal) against Ramoth Gilead. This war cost Ahab his life, and nearly cost Jehoshaphat his life too.

Later[163] Jehoshaphat was on the verge of another battle. This time, he was not the attacker, he was the one being attacked. He

---

163 2 Chronicles 20.

was also, as far as we can tell, in the weaker military position. So maybe with the memory of the previous battle where He had almost come a cropper still in his mind, Jehoshaphat adopted a very different approach to the impending confrontation.

This time He first called a fast and engaged in intense prayer.[164] Then he again sought out the voice of a prophet.[165]

Through the prophets, God asked him to lay down his weapons, to lay down the military power on which he had been able to rely on so many other occasions, and go with his troops to take up positions amongst the enemy and just stand firm. They were to stand firm and worship God with all their might.

I am sure you know the story well – how the worshippers went out in front of the armies and as they sang and worshipped the Lord, the attacking army effectively defeated themselves. The men in the opposing armies literally destroyed each other. Not one of them escaped death.

This story is incredible. It's incredible because it reminds us of the battle that we are in – and that as we engage in worship, we engage in a battle. It reminds us that through worship, battles are won not only in the spiritual realm, but in the very real realm of our everyday lives and situations. It's incredible because of the way it shows the completeness of God's power – the ability of God to intervene and turn a situation totally on its head. But all too often we forget the context of this story – which is one where disobedience that had robbed Jehoshaphat of God's power was replaced by obedient worship that ushered in the presence and power of God into his life.

And as I reflected on this story that day, I remembered that we are rarely presented with a formula in the Kingdom of God. More often we are presented with a challenge – to listen out for the footsteps of the Father and follow where He leads us.

Even if it means we need to get our faces to the floor for a while.

---

164 2 Chronicles 20:3–4.
165 2 Chronicles 20:15.

When we come to the end of ourselves: Worship in the testing times

Jehoshaphat was surrounded by impossible odds, a vast army that was way stronger than his at that time. He stayed sharp to the voice of the Lord through the spiritual disciplines of fasting and prayer, and in the face of overwhelming odds, he responded by laying down what little military power he had at his disposal at the time, and worshipping God.

When we come to the end of ourselves, when the odds against us have stacked up and we see no way through, then our obedience in worship is often tested to the limit.

I know many people who come to our church in Cheltenham in a place of real hardship, a place where they have come to the end of themselves. A place where the last tool in the bag is a song. When they do this it really makes a strong impression on me because I am so aware of the cost it means to them. But I am convinced that it is so often this obedient response of worship in the midst of challenge that seems to bring God's Kingdom to bear on their situations.

Some friends of ours in church recently went through a hugely testing time. Having previously lost a child in pregnancy, they found that their next pregnancy was also seriously at risk at around twenty-three weeks. There was a danger that they would lose not only the child but the mother too if they didn't agree to have the baby delivered by surgery at an age that meant survival was very, very unlikely. Their daughter was born and weighed only one pound.

The weight of half a bag of sugar.

It was a very distressing time for the family and a time when our church seriously got down on its knees and prayed.

The father, one of my friends and part of our worship team, came to our monthly worship team meeting and shared how things were going, and through the tears he explained how he wanted us as a team, not only to stand beside him and pray, but to stand with him and worship. So on that evening, the memory of which will probably never fade over the years, we all stood together as a team and worshipped alongside a friend whose wife was in hospital with a daughter whose life hung by a thread. It was a huge testimony for me of the obedience of my friend to allow his "Yes" in worship to build a platform for God to move in power. Of course, in that moment we didn't know what the outcome would be.

My friend's wife tells how, in those very hard times while her daughter was fighting for life in the incubator beside her, she also turned to praise. She recalls how hard it was to find peace in the hospital room with so many machines linked up to the various babies in the ward, all beeping and firing off regularly. She talks of how she not only worshipped over her own daughter, but also how she worshipped over the other babies in the ward – and when the words ran out she carried on singing in tongues.

This mother was of Hindu origin and she remembers one particular evening where she was worshipping in tongues over the babies in the ward. As she sang, she says how the ward grew peaceful, and silent. The machines all quietened down. One of the nurses came back in, and saw what was happening – a mother singing in a strange language, and the room becoming full of peace. Not being a Christian, this nurse initially thought that the mother was singing in her native tongue. This started a conversation about Jesus. How incredible, that in a moment of extreme distress and anxiety, this mother's obedience in worship not only brought peace into a very difficult place, but also potentially started a lost person on a journey towards Jesus.

As a church, many months later, we rejoiced as their baby came to be dedicated, and we celebrated again in worship, this time in a place of thankfulness that their daughter had not only survived, but was now fit and well and a part of our church family.

Of course, there are many stories that I could also tell that don't have such obviously happy endings, and I wish I could somehow explain why in some cases God works so evidently, and in other cases it seems that He doesn't. But I do know that His ways are higher than ours, and that His thoughts are above our thoughts and that in everything He works together for good for those who love Him.

The work of a worshipper: Having eternity in our worship

Are you convinced yet?

Are you convinced that our first response to God, the first call on our lives is to love on Him, and that in that place where we love on Him we build a platform for Him to move in power?

Well, if you don't take it from me, take it from one of my heroes.

A. W. Tozer said this: "Out of enraptured, admiring, adoring, worshipping souls God does His work. The work done by a worshipper will have eternity in it."[166]

I have lost count of the number of times that I have been asked this question: Is our worship real? Is what you lead on a Sunday real? In fact, if you ask most people these days what they want from their faith, their church, their worship, their answer would be that they want it to be "real".

But ask them what real worship looks like, and they struggle to articulate it.

Sometimes people will question the lack of lament in worship and say that our worship can't be real – and there may be some truth in that.

Some people may look at the way we strive for technical excellence in the band arrangements we do and say that because it is good, then it isn't real – and there may be some truth in that.

Others may look at some of the people in my worship team

---

166 *Worship: The Missing Jewel of the Evangelical Church*, 1961.

and know that the lives they have lived that week haven't been perfect and so they question whether what happens on a Sunday is real – and there may be some truth in that.

Others may question why a church will have a comfortable, well-lit arena for its Sunday worship when there are homeless people bedding down in the alleyway outside and say that our worship can't be real – and there may be some truth in that.

However, for me, when asking the question, "Is our worship real?" the only question we really need to ask is this: "Are we doing what God is requiring of us? Are we making a choice to worship Him first?" People will always question our sincerity in worship from all sorts of angles, but for me, the only mark of its reality is its level of obedience.

I hear many, many calls for a new thing in worship these days. Some are waiting for the new sound. Some are waiting for the new rhythm. Some are waiting for the next big celebrity worship star. Some are waiting for the new poetry or liturgy. Some believe a fresh expression of church will help. Some people think a fresh theology of liberalism will help. Many people are even saying that they are bored with church and worship in our Western world.

However, amongst all of those voices which, I suspect, are more of a symptom of our consumeristic culture than anything else, I don't find many leaders saying, "Just do it."

Just worship.

Stop complaining about the quality of the sound system, or the lighting levels on stage, or the competence of the drummer, and just worship.

Stop waiting for the song-u-like, the band-u-like, the celebrity worship leader-u-like to be fed up to you on a Sunday morning, and just worship.

Stop waiting for the new expression of creativity, the perfect melody, or the perfect lyric to fall in your lap, and just worship.

Even more so, stop waiting for your own life to be more

in order, more complete, more holy, more sorted, and just worship.

Stop waiting for your circumstances to be less painful, less messy, less disorganized, less complicated, and just worship.

Just do it.

Good old-fashioned discipline in worship. Good old-fashioned obedience in worship. Good old fashioned turning-up-week-by-week-and-lifting-your-voice-in-praise-to-God in worship.

Or as Mark Bailey puts it, "don't let what is wrong with you stop you worshipping what is right with God."

Just do it.

This is the most sure-fire way for all of us to know the touch of God's heart as people, as churches, as communities, as nations: to intentionally and obediently open up our own hearts and sing to God.

Just do it.

If we were all to come every week to church to worship our socks off, as an act of faithful obedience, then I think we would see an outpouring of the Kingdom of God like never before.

So just do it.

Love on God.

Because surely this is the starting point for everything?

Coram Deo: Living life to the face of God

I am not really bothered what people think about my personal reputation, or what my legacy will be when I hang up my worship-leading boots – if indeed that will ever happen. However, I would like my church to be known as a church that loves on God before anything else. I also hope that we will always be known as a church full of the presence and power of God.

And I would like to think that by now I have convinced you that these two hopes that I have for my church are inextricably linked – held together by the thread of obedience.

Of course, this raises a couple of questions: "How do we know that God is present?" and even if we can know that, "How does the presence of God manifest itself amongst us?" or again, "What does a presence-shaped person or community look like?"

My online dictionary defines "presence" as: "the state or fact of being present, as with others or in a place; attendance or company; immediate vicinity; proximity; the quality or manner of a person's bearing; personal appearance or bearing; of noteworthy appearance or compelling personality; a divine or supernatural spirit felt to be present."[167]

In the Old Testament, "presence" is a translation of the Hebrew *liphne*, which literally means "to the face of". As my friend Brian Howell says, biblically presence is not simply being around God, but being in respect to Him – that is, being orientated towards Him, or *Coram Deo*, "to the face of God". As R. C. Sproul puts it, "To live *Coram Deo* is to live one's entire life in the presence of God, under the authority of God, to the glory of God."[168] So, in order to form a conclusion to this chapter, I have searched the Scriptures, and this is what I have found that they say about the presence of God, the way it manifests itself, and what people and communities look like when they live *Coram Deo*:

In Genesis 1 it hovered over the waters;
in Exodus 3 it was a burning bush;
in Numbers 9 it was a cloud that moved from place to
    place;
in Isaiah 3 it is described as glorious;
in Psalm 89 it is described as light;
in Hosea 6 it is described as spring rain;
in Nahum 1 the earth trembled at it;
in Psalm 5 the arrogant couldn't stand in it;
in Acts 10 people listened to the voice of God in it;

167 http://dictionary.reference.com
168 *In the Presence of God*, Nashville: Word Publishing, 1999.

in Isaiah 26 people in agony cried out in it;

in Leviticus 9 and 10 God's fire came out of it;

in Psalm 9 nations were judged in it;

in 1 Thessalonians 3 people found joy in it;

in Joshua 18 and 19 people made big decisions in it;

in Psalm 18 hailstones and thunderbolts flew out
    from it;

in 1 John 3 people found rest in it;

in Psalm 41 those with integrity were allowed to
    remain in it;

Samuel grew up in it.

In Psalm 90 people were convicted of their sins by it;

in Deuteronomy 27 people rejoiced in it;

in Jeremiah 23 the disobedient were thrown from it;

in Luke 1 the angel Gabriel stood in it and spoke of
    good news;

in Deuteronomy 19 disputes were settled by men
    standing within it;

in 2 Kings 17 those who worshipped false idols were
    removed from it;

in Hosea 6 the injured and wounded were revived in it;

in Genesis 27 people blessed other people in it;

in Ezekiel 46 people worshipped in it;

in Deuteronomy 4 people were led by it;

in Deuteronomy 18 people served in it;

in 1 Chronicles 29 people ate and drank with great joy
    in it;

in 1 Thessalonians 3 people's hearts were strengthened
    in it;

in 2 Chronicles 6 people made their requests to God
    in it;

in Psalm 31 people found shelter in it;

in Psalm 16 people found pleasure in it;

John had the mother of all dreams in it.

In Deuteronomy 12 people brought their gifts into it;
in Deuteronomy 16 people made sacrifices in it;
in 2 Peter 2 angels watched what they said in it;
in 2 Chronicles 20 people cried out in distress in it;
in Deuteronomy 29 people made promises in it;
in Lamentations 2 people poured out their hearts in it;
in 2 Chronicles 34 God listened to the cries of His
    people in it;
in Psalm 139 David found it would be everywhere
    he went;
in 1 Corinthians the unbelievers fell down on their
    faces and worshipped in it;
in Habakkuk 2 people were silent before it;
in 2 Samuel 6 David danced with abandon before it;
in Psalm 84 we learn that a moment in it is better than
    anything else the world has to offer.

And one day all the saints will worship in it.
Forever.

Chapter 8

The One We Worship

THE GLORIOUS CHRIST

Simon Ponsonby

As I was writing this very chapter, I received an email from a fellow minister who I didn't know personally, and who didn't know I was writing this project, but who wanted to unburden himself and, for some reason, wanted to do so at me! He had attended a large summer Christian conference, and had enjoyed much of it, but he was uncomfortable with the "worship" times. He said that in years gone by, he had been particularly struck by the Christ-centred, cross-centred themes in worship, but in recent years, had observed a shift from focusing on Jesus and His work as the subject, to singing about our experiences of it. It was a matter of emphasis, for clearly to sing about the cross and Christ is to sing about our experience of such – but the focus, he felt, was in the wrong place. He said that he paid particular attention to the content, and observed that one worship leader in all his sets, cumulatively several hours of praise and worship, did not refer to the cross once – not once.

I wonder sometimes if a stranger walking into our churches, listening to our contemporary worship songs, would have any idea who we are singing to and why.

I don't believe this is just my pet peeve, I believe it is a fundamental biblical principle and practice. Worship must focus on God the Father *and* Jesus, reigning at the centre of heaven.[169]

---

169 Revelation 4:2–6; 5:6–14.

The missionary and church statesman, Oswald Sanders, once said: "Worship is the adoring contemplation of God as he has revealed himself in Christ..."

True worship centres on the one at the centre – Jesus.

There is a rare meteorological event known technically as a glory – it is a complete rainbow, not the usual arc or bow, but a full circle. Generally it is seen only by pilots in planes, caused by sunlight entering a cloud in two directions – diffracting, refracting through water droplets. I've always wanted to see one. I've taught about them, even shown pictures of them in church, and then last summer, flying home from holiday, I got to see one.

And it was truly glorious.

Glory is the self-disclosure of the being of God. It is God unveiled, God disclosed, God encountered.

The Swiss theologian Karl Barth wrote: "Glory – is the self-revealing sum of all divine perfections. It is the fullness of God's deity... self-expressing... self-manifesting... self-declaring – out-shining."[170]

Moses wanted to see a glory in Exodus 33:18. He tells God that His accompanying presence is not enough. He wants revelation, he wants intimacy, he wants true insight. He asks God, "show me your glory". And Moses, hiding behind a rock, is granted to catch just a glimpse of glory, the back of God. But the incredible, incredulous truth of Christianity is that God desired to reveal His glory in all its glory – not hidden in a rock, but fully displayed in the incarnation, in the person and work of Jesus Christ.

As St John said of Jesus: "We have seen his glory, the glory of the One and Only."[171]

And when we behold that glory, surely all we can do is give Him glory.

---

170 Karl Barth, *Church Dogmatics* Vol. 2, Part 1, Edinburgh: T&T Clark, 2004, p. 643.
171 John 1:14.

The pre-eminence of Christ
(Colossians 1:15–20)

He is the image of the invisible God, the firstborn over
all creation, for all things in heaven and on earth were
created by him – all things, whether visible or invisible,
whether thrones or dominions, whether principalities
or powers – all things were created through him and
for him. He himself is before all things and all things
are held together in him. He is the head of the body,
the church, as well as the beginning, the firstborn from
among the dead, so that he himself may become first in
all things. For God was pleased to have all his fullness
dwell in the Son and through him to reconcile all
things to himself by making peace through the blood
of his cross – through him, whether things on earth or
things in heaven.[172]

In these few famous verses, we have what is generally accepted as
being one of the earliest church creeds or hymns. Most scholars
recognize that it is a self-contained section, and the language and
style are not those usually seen in Paul's writings. The fact that
Paul cites it suggests that the Colossians were familiar with it –
indeed, I rather wonder if it isn't a hymn that actually originated
in the Colossian community, a song they themselves wrote.

Perhaps Paul is writing and asking: "You sing this song, but
do you really understand and stand on its truth?"

We need look no further than this remarkable hymn for
a model, a template for our worship and our theology. It is a
crystal-clear Christological diamond – with precise facets that
refract and radiate the majesty of God in the person of Jesus.
Significantly, it says nothing about the humble, meek carpenter's
son, Jesus of Nazareth; it focuses on the cosmic, conquering King

---

172 Colossians 1:15–20 NET.

of heaven and earth, the Lord Jesus Christ. This is not to negate the glory of His incarnation, humiliation, crucifixion – but Paul's emphasis ought not to be missed.

It is said that the medieval master artist and sculptor, Michelangelo, was once asked by his pupil Raphael to comment on a portrait of Jesus he was painting. When Raphael was out at lunch, Michelangelo paid a visit to his studio to see the picture of Jesus. On his return, Raphael saw that Michelangelo had taken a brush and painted over the whole portrait the Latin word *AMPLIUS*. He meant, "Make Jesus larger, bolder, more prominent, outstanding." Raphael's Jesus was too small; a pocket-sized portrait is not good enough. And this may have been the mistake the Colossian church had made, and this is certainly the mistake the modern church makes.

One stand-out feature in this Colossian hymn is the fourteen personal-pronoun references to Jesus, and the complete absence of any reference to us. True worship focuses on Jesus. It really is all about Him, and all this is for Him, for His glory and His fame; it's not about me or you. While there is a place to express our personal experience of meeting this Jesus, that should be done and sung in such a way as to crown Him, for His renown. He, Jesus, is the centre and subject of worship.

This hymn of praise to Christ is polemical. It sharply challenges the false theology creeping into the Colossian church – the early Gnosticism, the old-fashioned "New Age". This heresy undermined the incarnation by making Jesus neither God nor man. Driven by a Greek dualistic philosophy which drove a wedge between the divine and the human, this heresy asserted that, because God is Spirit, He is necessarily utterly distant and divorced from all created matter – which is evil, the product of wicked demi-gods, emanations that evolved further and further from God. Consequently, and contrary to apostolic truth and biblical revelation, this heresy claimed that Jesus was neither fully God nor fully man – but partly God and partly man. Because matter is evil, Jesus, who bore the spark of the divine, could not have truly taken human flesh. They claimed that when He walked He left no footprints in the sand – he only "appeared" human. But equally and oppositely, because He physically appeared on the fallen, evil, material earth and associated with its inhabitants, He couldn't be truly God. This heresy resulted in a Jesus who was too human to be God, and too godly to be human, and therefore unable to bridge the gulf between the two. But Scripture records that Jesus was *vere deus, vere homo*: truly God and truly man, God for man and man for God.

Jesus' divinity

He is the image of the invisible God. Jesus is the seen and unseen God, the invisible made visible.[173]

Paul uses the Greek word *eikon*, which referred to an exact copy or portrait, and was the term used by the famed Jewish philosopher Philo to describe the *Logos*, the divine mind. It was the term employed by Jews to describe Wisdom, the human-ward side of God.[174]

"In him all the fullness of God dwelt" is repeated with the additional phrase, "in bodily form". Jesus did not just have a spark of the divine, a special anointing, merely a hotline to God. Jesus had all of God's all-ness in Him. And in the Greek, all means all.

God "dwelt" in Christ, and Christ dwelt among us.[175] This concept of "dwelling" had particular force in the Old Testament, where the people were to dwell in the land and God was to make His dwelling in the temple.[176] This dwelling was not a nomadic passing through, a superficial acquaintance, a temporary habitation. God would reside with them. And now, in Christ, God comes to dwell, not in a temple of bricks, but a temple of flesh: corporeal, visceral, real, human.

God comes in person, as a person to be with persons. He is

---

173 Colossians 1:15.
174 *The Wisdom of Solomon* 7:26.
175 John 1:14.
176 Deuteronomy 12:5.

not distant, not absent, not indifferent, He is fully present and accounted for humanity.

He is before all things (verse 17). Jesus was before all else was. There never was a time when He was not. His beginning was eternal, a beginning before beginnings. He is the beginning (verse 18). Genesis commences its history of the universe with the famous words: "In the beginning God", so this hymn to Christ echoes this theme: "In the beginning Jesus"!

There was an idea in the first few centuries among some, which was quickly rejected as heresy, called Adoptionism. This notion claimed Jesus was a good human, a perfect human, whom God at His baptism filled with His Spirit in a special way. At this point Jesus was graced, adopted, elevated, brought into the family of God.

But Adoptionism is not the testimony of Christ about Himself: "before Abraham was born I was". Adoptionism is not the testimony of the prophets: "Unto us a child is born, unto us a Son [who already was] is given." Adoptionism is not the testimony of the apostles, who recorded that the eternal Word became flesh, God and blood wed in virgin's womb – the God of infinite contraction and condescension.

If the heresy of Adoptionism was to reduce Jesus' divinity, the alternative heresy is to reduce his humanity – making him only "appear" human (as the Docetists claimed). But Jesus the eternal Son of God became Jesus of Nazareth, the very real temporal, corporeal Son of Man. And this Jesus is the one we worship, not a man who became God, but God who became man, to bring all men to God.

God for man, man for God.

Jesus' creativity

For by him all things were created, in heaven and on earth, visible and invisible, whether thrones or dominions or rulers or authorities.[177]

---

177 Colossians 1:16.

The so-called Gnostics were a spiritual stream in the later first century who made much of the realm of the invisible over the visible, made much of hierarchies of spiritual angelic beings. And these ideas were influencing the church at Colosse – and these ideas were abstracting people from the centrality of Jesus. Spiritual, mystical, heavenly beings were all fascinating – these Christians were in danger of going off with the fairies. But Paul reminds them that their Jesus rules over all spiritual powers and authorities. He is at the top of the tower of their angelic or demonic hierarchies because not only was He before them, but He created them.

All beings, whether spiritual or natural, visible or invisible, were created by Jesus. He is the authority of authorities, the power of powers, the creator of all creation.

Our brightest scientists can make stem cells or clone sheep, but that's just manipulation. We cannot make something out of nothing. That's creation. Jesus can and did create. The cosmos was created by Him and for Him – for His glory, pleasure, and purpose. We can send rockets to the moon but Jesus can make the moon and a billion others like it.

The genius of his day, the seventeenth-century theologian, mathematician, and philosopher Blaise Pascal rightly observed: "Jesus is the centre of everything and the object of everything – he that does not know that knows nothing about nature and nothing about himself."

"In him all things hold together."[178] Jesus sustains creation.

One of the great quests in physics is the so-called "unifying theory of everything" – the mathematical equation that holds together Newtonian physics and Einstein's relativity and quantum mechanics. This is Jesus – He is the mind behind what physicists name the Big Bang, He is the origin of the species, the missing link. In the classical world Atlas strained to hold up the heavens, Hercules strained to hold up earth's globe. But Jesus holds together all things – effortlessly.

178 Colossians 1:17.

This challenges Scientism, which seeks to understand the cosmos as an independent accident, without reference to a divine Creator. This challenges Pietism – whether Gnostics or ascetics who disdain God's good creation – valuing ideas, enlightenment, detachment, the spiritual over the natural. This challenges Pantheism – that subsumes the Creator into His creation, and causes the pagan to worship the made, not the Maker. This challenges Deism – which posits God as first cause, prime mover, but then does away with God, has God go away, so we can contemplate a world which God connects with only as a tangent to a circle.

The God we worship is the Creator God – the power, the wonder, the designer, the beginning and end of all.

Jesus' supremacy

In this hymn the focus shifts starkly from us to Him. Here we see that the fullness we corporately seek as church is the fullness that Jesus already possesses in Himself. Christ is pre-eminent over *all* things. The song unmistakably repeats the Greek word for "all" nine times. It is all about Him, all because of Him, all to Him.

Worship is not for us, not about us.

Jesus is the point of it, Jesus who is above all.

It's all for Jesus, all for Jesus.

The word "firstborn" (verse 15b) is not to be understood as meaning "created first", as the Jehovah's Witnesses have interpreted it. Indeed, the use of the term "firstborn" is not used biblically in the sense of chronological creation, but in the sense of primacy, priority, authority, pre-eminence.

Not born first, but coming first.

It was the word used of the eldest male, not the eldest child, in a family. It was used of Israel[179] who, as a people or nation, were definitely not the first. It was used of the Messiah[180] to speak not of His creation but His position. To say "firstborn" is to say, "first,

---

179 Exodus 4:22.
180 Psalm 89:27.

numero uno, el primero". Jesus was not "birthed" first in creation; he reigns as number one over creation. H. G. Wells, the famous historian and novelist, wrote of Christ: "Is it any wonder that to this day this Galilean is too much for our small hearts?"

He is the head of the body, the church.[181] The head is the authority, covering, protector. The nerve-centre, the command post. The source of all life, action, and decisions taken by the body. In his argument, Paul will say that this church "has lost connection with the Head, from whom the whole body... grows".[182] The church, departing from Christ's control, has become like a headless chicken – running around making a mess and dying.

Note the metaphor of church as body. The church is Christ to the world – we are His body, His presencing, His representation. What a privilege, and what a responsibility. This church is a body, not a hierarchy or an oligarchy – she is an integrated, mutual, reciprocal, dependent organism, where every member matters. Christ holds headship in His church: not popes, priests, pastors, prophets, or PhDs. And not "men only"! Jesus Christ is head. He is Lord. He is in charge of His body. He is the source and subject of everything we say and do as church – worship, discipleship, outreach, teaching, intercession – everything.

Finally, we must observe that the great hymn which celebrates the significance of Christ, does so in the context of our significance to Christ. The hymn of verses 15–20 which addresses who He is, is framed by His work, by what He has done on our behalf (verses 12–14, 20–22).

Both who He is and what He has done for us fill and thrill our worship.

The person and work of Christ

We ought to notice the tense employed by Paul – the "aorist" – referring to a completed, accomplished act, that has happened

---

181 Colossians 1:18.
182 Colossians 2:19 NIV

at one point. Now, tenses matter. If my wife Tiffany said, "I may love you" or "I once loved you", I would be worried – doesn't she love me today?! If Paul had written that we "may be saved" or "will be saved" – we might ask about our position and standing before Christ today. But Paul speaks of the work of Christ for us as being a finished fact – something already established, a deed done.

God's benevolence

The Father has qualified us.[183]

The Colossians had been disastrously influenced by these Gnostic ideas that appealed to a religious elitism. The divine spirit was divorced from the mere mortal by a great gulf, as matter evolved and emanated further and further away from pure spirit. That return to the divine, that traversing of the gulf, comes, claimed the Gnostics, not by God becoming man and dying for man's sins as a sufficient sacrifice and substitute, but by man being enlightened in his thinking, by special knowledge and mortifying mortal flesh through ascetic acts. Like a Swiss mountain where steep ascents are aided by ladders or ropes, so the Colossians were being encouraged to ascend the mountain to God on the basis of their gaining secret knowledge (the word "Gnostic" comes from the Greek *gnosis*, "knowledge"), secret passwords revealed to and through the spiritual ones, and through strenuous asceticism and mysticism. The cult influencing the Colossians basically reduced salvation to gaining special knowledge through personal effort.

"Wrong," resounds Paul. The cross and all its benefits flow from God's *a priori* decree, action, gift.

We don't qualify ourselves – He qualifies us!

He qualifies me. I am saved not because of what I learn or what I do, but because of who He is and what He has done. I am the beneficiary of His benevolent act. And that is why we worship. "He has qualified us", and that is who we worship – "He,

183 Colossians 1:12a.

who qualified us". If we had qualified ourselves, we could worship ourselves!

Our inheritance

We share in the inheritance of saints, in the kingdom of the Son he loves.[184]

Ancient Near-Eastern cultures operated on primogeniture. The oldest, firstborn son inherited all or most of the father's wealth. Jesus is God's beloved Son, the firstborn and heir to heaven. But staggeringly, that status is conferred on us. We have become beloved sons of God, heirs and co-heirs with Christ, firstborn inheritors with Him. Many siblings row over their inheritance but Jesus shares what is His birthright with all who are born again.

My father is an avid antique expert and collector. Often when I visit he will show me his latest acquisition and say: "One day, son, all this will be yours." I'm always tempted to say, "Go on *Cash in the Attic* or *Flog It*. Raise some money and give it to me now!" In Christ, God shows us heaven, and says, "One day, son, all this will be yours." That is why Paul could say, "No eye has seen, no ear has heard, no mind has conceived what God has prepared for those who love him."[185]

Our deliverance

He has delivered us from the powers of darkness. We were once in the grip of the evil one, who had ensnared us by tempting us to sin and imprisoned us in his vicious grip. Our lives were marked by demonic control, death and eternal condemnation. But God intervened. The Great Knight of Heaven came and slew the dragon that enslaved, and rescued his future bride.

Again, tenses here matter – He has delivered us: this is not a future hope but a present reality based upon a past event. Many live in fear of the enemy, bound by his whispers, accusations

---

184 Colossians 1:12b–13.
185 1 Corinthians 2:9 NIV.

and torments. But he is defeated – the chains that bound us have been severed, his grip has been prised off us. And we need reminding, and he needs reminding of this. *Christus Victor* – Christ is victorious! The Lamb has won.

Colossians 1:13 says we have been "transferred into the kingdom of his beloved Son." Not only have we been taken from the snare of the evil one's lair, but we have been transported to the kingdom of heaven. The slave is now free, the jail exchanged for a palace. From poverty to heavenly riches, from death to life. We all love stories such as *Cinderella, Oliver Twist* or *Les Misérables* where someone's fortune is reversed, where their predicament is transformed. There is a deep existential connection to these stories, reflecting an innate longing at the depths of our being. This "fairy tale" narrative is indeed the very real gospel – the story of God's love for us – the transformation of a life.

Convergence

In Jesus we have redemption, the forgiveness of sin (verse 21). We who were once alienated, hostile to God and evil, now are reconciled to God, presented holy, blameless, and above reproach (verse 22).

The Bible says man is a sinner, a rebel. God's holiness distances Him from sinful humankind. Sin brings a dislocation and a separation from God. God's righteousness demands satisfaction. A just judge must exercise justice and judge sin. For God to overlook sin is to act unrighteously. It would be to violate His very being. It cannot be done. Man is under the judgment of God; he stands in his sin, guilty and condemned.

But the last word is not judgment but grace, not justice but mercy. God's loving-kindness.

God acts to do what humanity cannot do: to fully pay for the debt of sin, to fully satisfy the justice of God's law. God in His love for us, longs for us, and so reaches out to redeem us from the consequences of sin and reconcile us to Himself.

Redemption (Greek *apolutrosis*) is a key theme in the Old Testament. It is what God did at the exodus from Egypt when He acted sovereignly and powerfully to bring out the Israelites from slavery. In the New Testament the term refers more to deliverance from debt. Deliverance from slavery in Egypt occurred when the avenging angel of death came in holy wrath to kill the firstborn of Egypt. But Israel, by faith, killed the firstborn lamb and put its blood on their door-frames.[186] When the angel of death came, it "passed over" the bloody wood. They, that night, were then redeemed into liberty. And this redemption, this escape from slavery, by appropriation of the Lamb's blood, is no mere metaphor. It is the means and mechanism for our own deliverance from slavery to sin, death and hell.

Through the shed blood of Jesus, and our trust in it, we are set free.

Having been redeemed, brought out of sin's slavery by the Lamb's blood, we are then brought into union with God. The Lamb who redeems is the Lamb who unites. Redemption leads to reconciliation (Greek *apokatalassois*, verses 20, 22). *Apokatalassois* was a term used of bringing together that which was divided. The joining of broken roads. The joining of two parties at war.

God in Christ "lassoes" us to Himself.

God's love is a bloody business (verse 20), but as Luther said, one drop of Christ's blood is worth more than heaven and earth. He spilled it for you.

This precious salvation – our redemption and our reconciliation – does not come cheap. It is a very costly gift, only possible through Jesus' substitution – in His body of flesh; through Jesus' propitiation – through His death. Christ, fully God and fully man, stands in the gulf before God and man – man for God, God for man. In His body the two become one!

But this stepping into our shoes, this substitution, was not done reluctantly. It pleased (Greek *eudokeo*) or delighted God

---

186 Exodus 12:7.

in Christ to do this, so persuaded was He by the prospect of spending eternity with us. God did what was necessary. As the author of the letter to the Hebrews says, Jesus, for the "joy" that was before him, endured the cross, scorning its shame. Jesus Himself said: "No one takes my life from me but I lay it down freely." Jesus, the Lamb of God who takes away the sins of the world, the reconciler, the redeemer, is no hapless victim, but a willing champion.

And now, by faith, trusting in this free gospel that cost us nothing, but cost God almost everything, we are reconciled and redeemed, and able to stand holy, blameless, without accusation (Colossians 1:22). This is God's gift; this is the church's foundation; this is the apostolic gospel; this is the world's hope.

In *The Lord of the Rings* Aragorn says to Gandalf: "You are our captain and our banner. The Dark Lord has Nine [kings]. But we have One, mightier than they: the White Rider. He has passed through the fire and the abyss, and they shall fear him. We will go where he leads." Jesus Christ is our captain, Jesus is our banner. He is Lord of Lords, King of Kings. Vicariously He passed through the baptism of fire at Calvary, and victoriously He rose, shattering every bond of evil.

And this is the Who, and this is the Why we worship.

Chapter 9

Moments of Closeness

RECAPTURING A SENSE OF WONDER IN WORSHIP

Neil Bennetts

Not long ago we took our two young girls, Lizzy and Sarah, to a show in London's West End. It was a tenth birthday treat for Lizzy, our eldest, and we went to see *Mary Poppins*. We don't get to London very often as a family, and this was the first time we had taken our girls to a major show, and so it was a real excitement for all of us.

I remember that for the first couple of scenes I was only really interested in how it was technically pxut together. I checked out the orchestra pit, and identified what instruments were there and who was playing what. I checked out the lighting rig and the PA system, and even worked out how they wired all the actors and singers up on stage. And as someone who is constantly suffering from the effects of crackling microphone leads, annoying feedback, and crashing computers as I lead worship, I was even quite pleased when the guy on the sound-desk seemed to mess up a couple of cues.

After around fifteen minutes I had got it nailed.

I understood how it was working. The big part of me that always needs to explain why and how things work was satisfied. I could relax and enjoy the rest of the show.

Of course, my daughters were approaching the show in a very different manner.

From the moment the curtain went up, they were transfixed. Their gaze never once moved away from the action on the stage. Their eyes were alive, their attention captured. I did try at one point to point out another piece of technical wizardry that I had spotted, but they seemed totally uninterested. They were totally engaged in the story that was unfolding before their eyes, and seemed totally uninterested in trying to work out how and why it was happening. They were enthralled.

Captivated.

Lost in it.

Way over our heads: The desire to explain everything

We live in a culture that seeks to explain everything. We have a massive compensation culture because we always want to know why something happened, and who is to blame when it all goes wrong. If we buy something we have to totally research the products and their prices; we look at reviews and reports before making our decision. When we go on holiday we spend hours on the internet comparing locations and prices and features before we commit.

It seems in-built in us that we need to know everything about it before we give ourselves to it.

And if you approach faith like me, then you are tempted to do the same. I increasingly spend time, and money, and effort reading the word of God, studying the Scriptures, reading books that help form my theology and provide a foundation for my life. And if you don't do this, let me encourage you to do it. The church will always be stronger where it has more people who are deeply rooted in the word of God.

But if you are like me, you may have also come to realize that the more you know about God, the more you find you don't know about Him. The more you discover, the more there is still to be discovered. The more God satisfies your hunger for Him, the more hungry you seem to get; the more treasure you have come to know, the more treasure there is yet to be plundered.

> Have you ever come upon anything quite like this extravagant generosity of God, this deep, deep wisdom? It's way over our heads. We'll never figure it out. "Is there anyone around who can explain God? Anyone smart enough to tell Him what to do? Anyone who has done Him such a huge favour that God has to ask his advice?" Everything comes from Him; everything happens through Him; everything ends up in Him. Always glory! Always praise!
>
> So here's what I want you to do, God helping you. Take your everyday, ordinary life – your sleeping, eating, going-to-work, walking-around life – and place it before God as an offering. Embracing what God does for you is the best thing you can do for Him. Don't become so well adjusted to your culture that you fit into it without even thinking. Instead, fix your attention on God. You'll be changed from the inside out. Readily recognize what He wants from you, and quickly respond to it. Unlike the culture around you, always dragging you down to its level of immaturity, God brings the best out of you, develops well-formed maturity in you.[187]

This passage in Romans is one of the most well-quoted passages in the Bible about worship. We may more normally recognize it from a different version – where we are encouraged to offer our lives "as living sacrifices, holy and pleasing to God."[188] But all too often we forget that Romans 12:1 starts with that word "therefore". It is a response to what comes before it, in Romans 11. There we find Paul talking about the wisdom of God

---

187 Romans 11:33 – 12:2 The Message.
188 Romans 12:1.

as being "way over our heads".

Indescribable. Unexplainable. Unmeasurable. Unpredictable. Unquantifiable.

Way over our heads.

We'll never figure it all out.

Don't you find this slightly strange? That we are being asked to worship a God – give Him our sleeping, eating, going-to-work, and walking-around lives – give ourselves whole-heartedly to a God who we will never be able to fully describe, explain, measure, predict, or quantify.

Take a long, hard look. See how great He is – infinite, greater than anything you could ever imagine or figure out!

> He pulls water up out of the sea, distills it, and fills
> up his rain-cloud cisterns. Then the skies open up
> and pour out soaking showers on everyone. Does
> anyone have the slightest idea how this happens? How
> he arranges the clouds, how he speaks in thunder?
> Just look at that lightning, his sky-filling light show
> illumining the dark depths of the sea! These are the
> symbols of his sovereignty, his generosity, his loving
> care.[189]

Like any father, I have high hopes for my children and what they may achieve in life, but I love the fact that they were able to go to that show in London and get lost in the wonder of it all from the outset. Next time we go, I suspect they will be more inquisitive because that is all part of their journey of life, and so important. I also hope that as they travel their own journey of faith they will become people who will study the word deeply for themselves, that they will become people who will always be prepared to give an answer to everyone who asks them to give the reason for the hope that they have.[190]

But alongside that, I hope that they will never lose the

---

189 Job 36:27–31 The Message.
190 1 Peter 3:15.

wonder of worship.

That they will be happy to stand before God and not know everything.

To live in the wonder of God.

Even to get lost in it.

31 billion attempts at the impossible: Our insatiable hunger for information

Here in the twenty-first century, the world has access to more information than ever before. In fact, a recent study suggested that the amount of information contained in one week's worth of *The New York Times* is broadly equivalent to the amount of information someone in the eighteenth century would have access to in their entire lifetime. In our search for information, there are something like 31 billion Google searches every year. Yet here in the West, despite the fact that we have access to more information than ever before in the history of the world, we probably have less worshippers than ever before.

When God appeared to Moses in the burning bush and told him that he should go and lead the children of Israel out of Egypt, Moses asked, "Why me?" And God said, "I will be with you."[191] When Moses asked God for His name so that he could tell people who had sent him, God said, "I am who I am."[192] Moses was asking for information, and God was giving Him a person – Himself. It seems that God wanted to send Moses out on this incredible mission armed not so much with a formula but with faith; to set out on a journey not so much with a plan but with a purpose; to set out on his journey not so much with explanations, but with wonder.

Not formula but faith, not a plan but a purpose, not explanations but wonder.

You see, God was primarily after Moses' heart, and it seems

191 Exodus 3:11–12.
192 Exodus 3:14.

that God knew that to capture his heart, explanations were not going to be enough.

I am often intrigued by what drives some of the great pioneers in history. People who explored unexplored lands, unconquered mountains, or uncharted seas. Those who went up Everest, went to the north and south poles, or landed on the moon. They were people who prepared themselves for the journey with everything possible, who studied geography and geology, patterns of weather, and the movement of the planets. They were people who were as well prepared as they could be. Their lives depended on such things. But my guess is that it wasn't what they knew that drove them to do what they did, but what they didn't know.

Even if I had every answer to every question in the universe, I'm not sure that this would cause me to worship all the more. I'm really not sure that it would. Because one of the reasons I think I worship God is not just because of what I do know about Him, but because of what I don't. The more I see, the more I think there is to see. The more my hunger gets satisfied, the more hungry I get. In fact, it is possibly what I don't know about Him – the mystery that surround Him – that propels me into a life of devotion and service and worship.

Or is it just me?

The unmistakable fragrance of the wonderful: The wonder of God in creation

There are many so-called wonders of the world. Depending on who you ask or what book you read, or which period of history you are studying, then there are many lists. Depending on what you read, there were the original seven wonders (425 BC): the Great Pyramid of Giza; the Hanging Gardens of Babylon; the Statue of Zeus (at Olympia); the Temple of Artemis (at Ephesus); the Mausoleum of Maussollos (at Halicarnassus); the Colossus of Rhodes; the Lighthouse of Alexandria. Then there are the seven wonders of the Middle Ages (the sixteenth century): Stonehenge; the Coliseum; the Catacombs (at Kom el Shoqafa); the Great Wall of China; the Porcelain Tower of Nanjing; the Hagia Sophia (in Istanbul); the Leaning Tower of Pisa.

When I look at these – although I have not seen all of them in real life – I am amazed at the ingenuity that brought them into being, the commitment and pursuit of excellence that erected them, constructed them, built them. But I would never say that any of them really capture my heart. And when I see how we have built an island in Dubai I am impressed, but I am not filled with wonder. Quite possibly this is because I know that somewhere, there is a set of plans, a series of reports, a file full of calculations that explains each of them fully.

Then you come across the seven natural wonders of the world: the Grand Canyon; the Great Barrier Reef; the Harbour of Rio de Janeiro; Mount Everest; the Polar Aurora; the Paricutin Volcano; Victoria Falls. And in comparison to the man-made wonders, these things are so stunning, so incredible that I never really get close to understanding how they came to be as they are. I may try to understand, I may search for answers, but at the end of that search, I am normally left with even more questions than when I first started. There is no master plan, no set of engineer's reports, no file of calculations that can fully explain them, completely quantify them, nail their creation down. They have that unmistakable quality that keeps us returning to gaze at them again and again: they have the unmistakable fragrance of the wonderful.

My wife loves the coast, the sea. She was brought up in a little town called Carrickfergus in the Northern Ireland, on the shore of Belfast Loch. When we met, we both were living in Norwich, in the east of England, and we took regular trips to the beautiful Norfolk coastline. When we came to Cheltenham and got married, she came to a place in the UK that is almost as far as you can get from any beach, coastal path, or view of the ocean. It has been a sacrifice for her, I know that. Because she loves being by the sea. She loves the beauty and strength and vastness of it all. And of course I share it, I love it too.

And I'm sure one of the reasons we both love it is because of its mystery. The fact that the depths and power in the ocean, despite humankind's attempts to understand them, are still very unpredictable and unmeasurable, and actually still relatively unscarred by man's presence on the earth. So often we stand on the shoreline, looking out across the ocean and seem to connect with something – something way beyond what our minds can explain. Our eyes may scan across the coastline and see the wonderfully constructed and intricate layout of the houses and the hotels and the parks – the mark of mankind's occupation of the land – and we may be impressed. But very soon we defer back to the sea and we see how relatively untamed it is, how powerful it is, how raw it is, how captivating it is. The creation of the Creator calling out to His created.

Now living where we do in Cheltenham, in an equally beautiful part of the country but far from the sea, we have to be ever more intentional about making trips there. Whether that's in our choice of summer holidays or in our journeys to visit friends, we have to make the effort to get to those places where we can get a sea view, walk on a coastal path, or wander about on the beach, where we can drink in the beauty around us.

You see, what I've found is, although I will never be able to unpack and explain all the mysteries of God, I can put myself purposefully in places where I can experience them, embrace them, and allow Him to capture my heart through them.

We see so much of King David's life and journey in faith documented in the Psalms, and one of the themes that weaves its way through them is creation, the works of God's hands, and how they are a constant reminder to David of God's faithfulness. One of the most well known is Psalm 121:

I lift up my eyes to the hills – where does my help
come from? My help comes from the Lord, the Maker
of heaven and earth.[193]

And we read in Psalm 125:

Those who trust in the Lord are like Mount Zion,
which cannot be shaken but endures for ever. As the
mountains surround Jerusalem, so the Lord surrounds
his people both now and for evermore.[194]

Psalm 8 says this:

O Lord, our Lord, how majestic is your name in all the
earth! You have set your glory above the heavens. From
the lips of children and infants you have ordained
praise because of your enemies, to silence the foe and
the avenger. When I consider your heavens, the work
of your fingers, the moon and the stars, which you
have set in place, what is man that you are mindful of
him, the son of man that you care for him?[195]

Creation is one of those things that I find can help us on this
journey in wonder. When we see the power and majesty of His
creation, we hear a message of love as His children, a constant
reminder of His commitment to us. My wife and I find that
going to the coast helps us to get everything in perspective, to
glimpse more of the wonder of God. One of the tragedies of the
damage we are doing to our planet is that we are losing parts of
creation that are gifts to us, reminders to us of God's goodness
and faithfulness. I don't know about you, but I can cope with
things getting a little warmer, and I can cope with some slight
reshaping of our coastline. What I find difficult to cope with is

193 Psalm 121:1–2.
194 Psalm 125:1–2.
195 Psalm 8:1–4.

the permanent removal of things on the earth that were created by God as a gift to us – and the removal of which will certainly make our lives poorer.

The most wonderful thing in the world: The wonder of worship

But for me, there is one place that is more significant, more important, more wonder-inducing than the greatest piece of creation, the most magnificent ocean view or the most breathtaking mountain view.

And that is the wonder of meeting with God in worship.

The meeting of God in worship.

Whether that's as we sit alone in our study, our office, our favourite coffee shop. Whether we join with a couple of friends in someone's home midweek. Or whether we join with thousands upon thousands at a big conference. For me, the greatest wonder in life is the wonder that we can meet with God, encounter God, experience His manifest presence.

This, for me, is true wonder.

A couple of years ago, our church managed to get hold of a number of video clips from our mission partners around the world. We didn't really plan it, but it just sort of happened that in the video footage we got back from many of those places, there were many clips of people worshipping.

We had clips of a church in Burundi meeting in a tin shed in the middle of Africa. We had clips of a few hundred people worshipping with incredible passion in a church building in Sri Lanka. We had some clips of a small number of people gathered in a basement in Afghanistan singing a few songs by the light of candles. It was incredible and humbling to see so many people – often in situations which were dangerous and challenging – gathering together for worship. In most cases, the musicianship of those leading was pretty dubious. The PA systems were limited or non-existent. And the songs were often songs written in the eighties that we in our church here in Cheltenham have long since discarded.

But as I watched these clips I was once again struck by the wonder I could see in the faces of the people singing. The wonder that, whatever their circumstances and situations, God was doing this: meeting with them, showing His face, pouring out His presence, showering down His favour.

As they sang.

As they worshipped.

And I sometimes think that in our Western churches we have lost a bit of this. That in our desire to understand worship, to go on courses and be trained, to learn about band dynamics and chord structures and the like, along the way we have lost a little of the wonder, lost a little bit of the mystery. Don't get me wrong, I think all of these practical things are important. I still continue to put a whole heap of my own effort into the equipping of others, in training musicians and worship leaders. It is so important. But what I never want to do is let that achievement of skill, understanding and explanation allow the flame of wonder to start to flicker.

Because it is still so important that we are able to stand in the presence of God and not know everything.

To live in the wonder.

To even get lost in it.

Because it captivates our hearts, and at the end of the day, more than anything, God is after our hearts.

You know, I have many things that I believe I need to do as a worship leader. I need to be theologically deep. I need to be creatively risky. I need to be compassionately pastoral. I need to work hard at the practicalities, the dynamics, the skills. But if my church isn't coming to worship and finding themselves lost in a little bit of wonder at what they are doing when they sing, then I have probably failed in my duties.

Moments of closeness: Growing in wonder through encounter with God

I try to know everything I can about my daughters. I try to know what motivates them, what inspires them, what they like, what they dislike. My wife and I purposely invite their school friends around to the house because we want to know the people who are influencing them day by day. We always make sure we go as a couple to their parents' evenings and school concerts and music events. We want to know as much as we can about them, so we can fulfil our parental role as well as we possibly can.

A couple of years ago, my eldest daughter had an accident. She is absolutely fine now, and actually if I look back at the incident, it is probably quite similar to what many parents have to go through with their growing, energetic children. But for a moment our world was shaken. Lizzy, while trying to enact a particularly challenging move on her bike, fell. And as she fell, the bike swivelled and she landed on top of the end of one of the handlebars. She was in agony, and after a little while we decided to take her to the hospital.

Eventually we got seen by a doctor, who immediately sent her for a scan to check for any internal damage. The results came back and she was immediately sent for a further scan. Of course, at this stage we feared the worst. One scan for a check was OK. To be sent back immediately for another one rang all sorts of alarm bells. Then when the second scan came back they said Lizzy would have to be taken to the hospital in Gloucester a few miles away because they thought she may need an operation. They feared that the handlebar had punctured her duodenum.

And that, they said, didn't get better by itself.

So we followed the ambulance to the hospital and spent a very worrying couple of hours waiting for the opinion of the consultant. Eventually they decided they didn't need to operate – which turned out to be the right decision – but we did spend a couple of very worrying days with Lizzy in hospital, with Susie and I staying by her bedside as she recovered. Any parent who has been through the hospitalization of their child knows how tough and emotionally draining it can be. Our daughter, thankfully, only had a relatively minor accident, and has since fully recovered, but the stress and worry it caused us was incredible at the time.

A few days later, Lizzy came home, and after a couple more days' rest, we eventually decided it was time for her to venture out, and so I took her into town to one of our favourite coffee shops for a hot chocolate. I remember that morning so clearly. Only a few days after I had thought she was severely injured, I was wandering into town in the clear morning sun, with my arm around my precious daughter, seeing her smile and catching the sparkle in her eyes, and chatting warmly.

And my heart was captured.

However much I knew about her, however much I made sure she was being led in the right things, however much I made sure I knew her skills and her calling, however much I spent thinking about what she needed to succeed in life, however much I did all those things – nothing could compare with the wonder of that moment. That moment of closeness, those few precious minutes walking arm in arm into the centre of Cheltenham on a beautiful sunny morning. More than ever, moments like that propel me as a father into a lifetime of devotion towards her.

You see, we can, and should, try to find out as much as we possibly can about God. We have to do that. But nothing can replace those moments of closeness that we find in His presence.

Lost in the wonder of it all.

When we stand before God, and it is all right not to know everything.

A wonder-full church

No one likes a know-all, and the church is often perceived as pretending to have all the answers.

It's a dangerous impression to give. Because we don't, and we never will. So when we come together to worship, I wonder what impression we are giving to those who enter into our buildings, sit in our pews, lift their eyes and open their mouths and sing the words we project onto our video screens.

What do the words and content of our songs communicate? What does the way we worship say about who God is, who we are, and what journey we are on as His church? Do all these things speak of a people who feel they know all that they need to know, and have got to their destination already? Or do all these things speak of searching and hungry hearts, desperate to see more of God, desperate to see more of His Kingdom revealed, desperate to keep climbing the mountain to see what is up at the next ridge, desperate to get there because the view will be more breathtaking, more beautiful, more captivating than it was at the last stopping-point? Because for me, that is what keeps worship fresh – keeps me searching, keeps me following, keeps me singing.

Songwriters, when we write our next song, will we be content to use language that has been used often before, poetry that has been applied before, melodies that have been constructed before, or will we believe that the best is yet to come, that there is more expressive language yet to be used, more resonating poetry yet to be discovered, more beautifully crafted melodies yet to be created?

Church leaders, do we so fill our Sunday gatherings to the brim, measure the times of worship to the minute, leave no space for something unpredictable to happen, or do we construct our programmes with some margins in them in anticipation of the unanticipated?

Worship leaders, are we spending too much time trying to ensure that our songs explain God properly, rather than trying to make sure they reveal God more fully?

To those of us who are part of deciding how our churches look architecturally, have we lost the ability to reflect the greatness and wonder and mystery of God in our church buildings? The first person ever described as being filled with the Spirit is someone called Bazalel. He was an artisan. He was the one who was appointed to do the design work for the tabernacle in Exodus 31. He was "filled with the spirit, in understanding, in knowledge, and in all kinds of craftsmanship to make artistic designs for work with gold, sliver and bronze."[196] With such a rich heritage in church buildings and art that reflects the glory of God in all His creative power, some of our church buildings these days seem so dry and plain and uninspiring.

Maybe we have taken away too much of the structural beauty in our worship centres and reduced them to mere functional spaces, whereas when I read the whole biblical narrative I really believe that our buildings and sacred spaces are not primarily functional – they are part of our identity as the creative, glory-reflecting, Spirit-filled people of God.

Maybe we have come to deride – at our own expense – the place of symbols and sacraments, the arts and beautiful objects. Isn't it time we revisited this area – not to give prominence to the self-centred, insecure, aggressive warrior artists who have historically allowed their craft to deflect glory away from God onto themselves, but to encourage God-honouring, servant-hearted, Spirit-filled artists and designers who have learned the art of capturing the wonder and mystery of God and expressing it in ways that shine glory back onto God accompanied by the gaze of His people. Maybe we need to question our embarrassment about language and activity that we discard because we feel it would be inaccessible, when actually we may be robbing the church of its heritage and its ability to express the deep things of

---

196 Exodus 31:3–4, NET.

God to a world that is hungry for them.

There is a great story in Mark 9. Some of the disciples were arguing with the teachers of the law, and they had attracted a large crowd. There was a sick child, and the disciples were trying to deal with it, trying to heal the child. There was Kingdom activity that needed to happen, and it was proving to be a big challenge. We read that Jesus came down from the mountain where he had been with Peter, James, and John, and came to rejoin the rest of the disciples. And as Jesus came towards the crowd, we are told that they were "overwhelmed with wonder and ran to greet him."[197]

I love this description, this imagery: that a crowd of people were so overwhelmed with wonder that they ran to greet Jesus. What a great description of worship! What a great description of what our gathered worship should be like. Running towards Jesus with wonder. Not armed with information, but running with wonder. That's what I want our church to feel like when we gather together.

Have you ever wondered why the presence of God is so often described as a cloud? Like at the dedication of the temple in 2 Chronicles 5,[198] when the presence of the Lord fell as the people worshipped. Strange, isn't it? At the times when the presence of the Lord is heavy, it is often described as something that is mysterious, something that conceals things rather than reveals things. Something that seems to illustrate not so much what we can see, but what we can't.

A cloud.

It seems that when God's presence is strongest, He comes not only with a reminder of what we know, the revelation of His promise and faithfulness in our lives so far, but He also comes with an invitation to press into Him all the more. He comes with a promise that, however wonderful, glorious, incredible the things we have seen and heard and know thus far are, there is always

---

197 Mark 9:15.
198 2 Chronicles 5:13.

more to find, always more to know, always more to discover.

We in our churches and in our ministries need to live in wonder. We can't reduce our lives as worshippers to a set of procedures, creeds or profit-and-loss accounts. We need to linger in the cloud a little more – not always trying to explain it, manage it, control it, assess it. We need to pause in that place where things are mysterious and let the wonder grow.

It's what brings life alive.

Chapter 10

In Awe or an Eeyore?

GRUMBLING IN WORSHIP

Simon Ponsonby

Worship is a response to the revelation of God in our lives.

When we encounter God, the natural and necessary response is worship. But we can so easily fail to lift our eyes to God, and instead stay focused on ourselves, our needs, our pressures, our issues, our wants. When our gaze is God, our attitude is one of awe – when our gaze is on ourselves, we are inclined to be Eeyore.

Eeyore was A. A. Milne's creation – a bluish, slump-shouldered, grumpy, down-in the-dumps donkey – constantly fearful his tail would be lost or his house blown down. For Eeyore, every cloud had a black lining.

Listen to some of his self-pitying and sulks:

Life is a box of thistles and I've been dealt all the really thorny ones.

Good morning Pooh Bear, if it is good morning. Which I doubt.

Nobody minds, nobody cares. Pathetic, that's what it is. Pathetic.

"Eeyore, Christopher Robin is having a party" said Owl. "Very interesting" said Eeyore, "I suppose they will send me down the odd bits which get trodden on."

Many of us have a propensity to be like Eeyore, rather than live in awe.

My mum calls my dad "A religious Victor Meldrew" and my wife thinks I follow suit – grumpy, grizzly, at times cynical or self-obsessed. Always looking on the dark side.

Benjamin Disraeli, the notable Victorian prime minister, amusingly recorded that "When I meet a man whose name I cannot remember, I give myself two minutes, then if that's a hopeless cause, I simply say, 'And how is the old complaint?'" Instantly, this question was guaranteed to make the other individual like him, feeling here was one who knew and cared about their condition, and this would cause the person to open up. Disraeli understood well the human condition and the propensity in many to be self-interested and overly obsessed about one's own, often petty issues.

The true worshipper has taken their eyes off themselves and turned their gaze to God. Regardless of trials and troubles, they are caught up by the splendour, the majesty, the glory, the goodness of God.

The psalmists repeatedly show us a movement from wallowing in self-pity or anxiety about circumstances, and consciously lifting their face to Father God – in whose presence their predicaments take true perspective.

The unmistakable Mr Eeyore

The Israelites repeatedly saw the hand of God outstretched in the most unimaginable, unprecedented fashion. Though constant witnesses to, and recipients of, miraculous gracious provision, they constantly chose to live like Eeyore, rather than live in awe.

A term which we constantly see attached to them, throughout Exodus and Numbers, is the Hebrew word *tlunott*, meaning "murmuring, complaining, grumbling". A peevish, quarrelling, irritated, moaning. At virtually every stage of their journey, following their exodus from Egypt, we see this Eeyore character trait betray them:

- At the Red Sea[199] the Israelites complain: "Is it because there are no graves in Egypt that you have taken us away to die in the wilderness?... Leave us alone that we may serve the Egyptians..."
- At the wilderness of Shur[200] the Israelites grumble against Moses because the waters are bitter: "What shall we drink?"
- At the wilderness of Sin[201] the Israelites grumble against Moses: "Would that we had died by the hand of the Lord in the land of Egypt, when we sat by the meat pots and ate bread to the full, for you have brought us out into this wilderness to kill this whole assembly with hunger."
- At Rephidim[202] they grumbled against Moses, wanting water: "Why did you bring us up out of Egypt, to kill us and our children and our livestock with thirst?"

This self-pitying, ungrateful, faithless complaint is echoed at Taberah[203] and at the edge of the promised land at Kadesh Barnea.[204]

The English literary figure, J. B. Priestley, once wrote: "I have always been a grumbler. I am designed for the part – sagging face, weighty upper lip, rumbling resonant voice – money couldn't buy a better grumbling outfit." Israel wandering through the wilderness must have worn a grumbling outfit just like that!

What do we make of all these incidents of ungrateful whinging and whining? In every case, it is their flesh dictating their attitudes. They are driven by their appetites for gratification.

---

199 Exodus 14:11–12.
200 Exodus 15:22–25.
201 Exodus 16:2f.
202 Exodus 17:3.
203 Numbers 11:4f.
204 Numbers 14:2f.

186 NOW TO HIM

Their priorities are the reverse of Christ's: "Man shall not live by bread alone, but by every word that comes from the mouth of God."[205] In every case, they fail to learn from God's provision for them previously and fail to simply trust God to go on providing. In every case, they slander God's nature and character and purposes in bringing them out of Egypt – they think He wants them to die in the wilderness! In every case their criticism, while levelled at God's appointed leader, Moses, was ultimately a criticism against God.[206]

In every case, Israel had a total loss of perspective – they failed to remember just how terrible slavery in Egypt was and they bizzarely rewrote their horror story in Egypt as some sort of holiday.

In every case they put God to the test – but unbeknown to them, He was putting them to the test and they failed (Exodus 15:25; 16:4). In every case they fail to show gratitude to God for previous provision and faith in God for future provision. In every case, they show they don't actually know the God who has elected and graced them.

Most amazingly, in every case God hears and answers their requests and indeed gives them more than they asked or expected – certainly more than they deserved! Thus, in Exodus 14:12, as they come to the Red Sea, with the Egyptians in hot pursuit, what they want is deliverance; but not only do they escape the Egyptians through the Red Sea, they also see all their Egyptian enemies killed – no threat remaining whatsoever. In Exodus 15:24 in the desert they crave water; but not only do they get sweet water instead of bitter, they also are promised that they will never be sick. In Exodus 16:3–15 they crave bread and meat, but not only do they get manna and quail, they also get God's glory standing before them. In Exodus 17:1 they want water again – but not only do they get water, they also get God standing before them (Exodus 17:6).

---

205 Matthew 4:4.
206 Exodus 16:7; Psalm 78:19.

God does exceedingly more than we can ask or even imagine.

Their grumbling is met by God's grace.

Are you an Eeyore or do you live in awe of God?

I confess I'm a bit of an Eeyore. On holiday one summer in France, I asked my son Joel, who was about five at the time, what he liked best about having me around instead of at work. He replied: "That you buy me treats – ice-creams." I then asked: "Is there anything you don't like about having me around?" I anticipated him answering in the negative: "No, Dad, when you are here it's all awesome." But instead, and as quick as a flash came back: "You're always grumpy."

Ouch!

Out of the mouths of babes 'n' infants!

I think Jesus had a right to be an Eeyore. He left the incomprehensible glory of heaven for a cattle-feeding trough in a stable. He self-limited his omniscience for infant ignorance – the eternal Word needing to be taught his ABCs by mother Mary. Jesus denied his omnipotence for impotence – the Creator and Sustainer of the universe needing to learn to crawl, then walk. Jesus left the reverence of the angels for the rejection of men. He left the throne of God for the whipping-post of men. Yes, Jesus had a right to grumble, murmur, complain, bemoan his lot – but no, never, not once! He willingly takes his bitter cup and with grace, trust and acceptance says, "Into your hands I commit my Spirit."

The ungrateful, unfaithful Mr Eeyore

With the exception of the Song of Moses,[207] there is no other recorded praise by the people of Israel in these chapters. Was there ever such a lack of gratitude for such a wealth of grace? They are the most ungrateful, unappreciative, selfish, miserly people since Adam, about whom not one word of thanksgiving,

---

207 Exodus 15.

worship, praise is ever recorded.

Let's just recap what God had done for them before they started murmuring:

- He had heard and heeded and responded to their cry of suffering;
- He had humiliated and decimated the cause of their years of suffering;
- He had delivered them from their slavery, breaking their bonds;
- He had laden them down with plundered gold, silver and goods.

God worked extraordinary miracles which should have had them speechless in awe, not murmuring like Eeyore. To cross the Red Sea in a night would mean the 2 million would have needed to be 5,000 abreast, over a width of 2 miles! If they crossed in pairs, it would require thirty-five days and nights! To feed and water 2 million folk[208] is like feeding a whole city! Water enough to drink, wash and water their livestock would require several million gallons a day! The US Army Quartermaster General has estimated that 1,500 tons of quail and manna would have been needed every day to feed them all.

All this God did for them and yet they were Eeyore, not in awe. There is barely a hint of praise, thanksgiving, gratitude or glory to God!

After God wipes out Egypt, we do see a song led by Moses, praising God for His mighty deliverance, but when Miriam and the ladies join in dancing in celebration (Exodus 15:20), the chaps can't be bothered! After each of the three times God responds to their murmuring, not once do they thank him for His kindness, generosity, and miraculous provision.

If only they had praised God, bringing to mind His faithfulness; if only that was a constant movement in their hearts and minds, constantly calling to mind His goodness

---

208 Numbers 1:46.

and faithfulness; then maybe they wouldn't have doubted His provision the next time they were in need.

The Russian novelist Dostoyevsky once said: "The best definition of man is 'the ungrateful bipod.'" How true of the Israelites and sadly, how true of us. How important it is that we keep rehearsing what God has done for us, praising Him for it, for that is His due! But it benefits us also. As we praise Him for His goodness, we re-visit, re-experience, re-appropriate it.

The Roman Catholic priest and spiritual writer, Brennan Manning, recalls one occasion when he was working on the rubbish dumps in Mexico. He gave a small gift of cash to a poor family who wrestled a living out of more privileged people's waste. This family were so blown away by this small token of generosity that in the next two days, Brennan received nine letters of gratitude from them. It seemed as if the family, every few hours, were so struck by their gift, that they had to give thanks. No doubt Brennan understood then that "It is far better to give than receive."

How often do we call to mind God's goodness to us and give Him thanks? If we only truly appreciated what Christ has done for us in settling our debt to God, in slaying the demonic Egyptians of sin, death, hell, Satan – if only we realized how God has laden our arms with gold and silver, the riches of heaven, we would live in awe and never Eeyore again.

Not only ungrateful but unfaithful. Despite miracles and provision which should have elicited awe, they don't trust God, they think He lies.

God had made promises to them through Moses about what he was going to do: taking them out of Egypt, taking them into the land He swore to give their forefathers. And God, true to His word, has brought them out of Egypt, with a remarkable display of power. But, only two weeks out of Egypt and a few miles from Canaan, they doubt His word, doubt His promise, doubt His provision, doubt His power. They wonder whether this is all a trick: has He led us here to kill us? Despite the evidence before their eyes of gold, silver, livestock, dead enemies – they don't trust God. And each time they moan and groan, and each time God meets their needs, they still don't change, they still keep grumbling!

So what does God have to do to convince them He's trustworthy?

Die?

Paul, writing to encourage the church of God to be faithful, says: "He who did not spare his own Son but gave him up for us all, how will he not also with him graciously give us all things?"[209]

Do we believe this?

Does not the cross say at the very least, God can be trusted, God is with us, He is for us, He comes through for us.

We are so often like Israel! We fail to trust God. We suffer a sort of spiritual amnesia and soon forget every answer to prayer, every act for us by God. We so easily forget Calvary, so easily forget His goodness, faithfulness, loving-kindness.

I believe God wants us to come to Him like little children – not worried about such things as can He, will He? Just expectant and believing! My boys don't come home and say, "Is there any tea, can we afford supper, are you going to make me fast, what if the cupboards are empty, what if the cooker's bust, what if you want me to starve to death?" They simply say, "What's for tea, when's tea, can I have some more?"!

As their father, I love their trust in me to provide, and I love their joyful consuming of what I give them, and I love it when they thank me.

And I think God is a little like that too.

The unfruitful Mr Eeyore

We recently went on a two-week holiday in France, a gift of God through the generosity of friends. On that holiday Joel said I was grumpy.

---

209 Romans 8:32.

I moaned about everything.

It was France, not Switzerland.

They spoke French.

The weather was too hot.

The flies were too numerous.

The TV was too fuzzy.

The bed was too soft.

The sofa was too old.

The shower was too thin.

The sea was too wet.

After a week I was as miserable as sin!

Rather than thank God for His goodness, His generosity, the gift of a foreign holiday with spending money, I moaned and robbed me and my family of the gift. Perhaps I grumbled so much that even God got so fed up, He allowed my car exhaust to blow, and I humiliatingly had to roar all the way to the ferry, with all the passengers staring and blocking their ears.

I then proceeded to throw up for four hours coming back.

Marlene Dietrich said, "Grumbling is the death of love." I don't think our grumbling causes God's love to die, but it causes our love to die.

It costs us, it robs us.

Though God repeatedly met their needs, ultimately, failure to trust and be grateful robbed the Israelites of joy, peace, contentment, of enjoyment of God's presence. They were marked by anxiety, fear, depression, and *angst*!

For Eeyore, life always seems a chore!

For the Israelites, God in His grace provided for them.

Whenever their murmur was in the face of real need – facing enemies, facing lack of food or water – they failed the test of faith. But He didn't fail them.

But when they murmured for no reason, simply because they wanted onions and garlic or when they refused to enter the Promised Land, then they faced his wrath![210] He sent snakes and

---

210 Numbers 11:14.

fire among them and many were killed.

To the church, Jude 16 says, "The Lord will judge grumblers"; to the church, Paul writes, "We must not... grumble, as some of them did and were destroyed by the Destroyer";[211] to the church, James says, "Do not grumble... so that you may not be judged."[212]

When the Israelites murmured in Numbers 14:2, and said it would be better for them to have died in the wilderness rather than fight for the Promised Land, God said, "Your wish is my command!" Everyone would die in the desert over the next forty years. Graciously, He led them, fed them, and their shoes never wore out – but they never entered the place of promise. Their murmuring, grumbling and rebellion cost them Canaan.

The writer to the Hebrews wrote: "they were unable to enter [rest] because of unbelief. Therefore, while the promise of entering his rest still stands, let us fear lest any of you should seem to have failed to reach it."[213] It is not our eternal destiny of heaven that we forfeit by grumbling. That is guaranteed in Christ's blood. But by grumbling, we may forfeit, in this life and the next, many of the benefits that Christ purchased at Calvary.

Rather than be like Eeyore, fearing we are losing a tail, let us be like Winnie the Pooh, celebrating, joyful, and grateful: "Nobody can be uncheered with a balloon."

God has given us so much more than a balloon. Let us live in awe, not as Eeyore – rejoicing, thanking and trusting God.

---

211 1 Corinthians 10:10.
212 James 5:9.
213 Hebrews 3:19 – 4:1.

Chapter 11

A Church that Dances

ENGAGING IN PASSIONATE, SACRIFICIAL WORSHIP

Neil Bennetts

I was leading worship some while ago, and at one point during the evening, the sense of celebration was rising, the excitement was growing as we encountered God, and it got to the point where it seemed like a dance was in order. But while many of the worshippers on stage and in the congregation around me seemed totally at ease with the situation, I found myself totally ill-equipped to respond as I felt I should do.

Now you need to know something about me. I am very English. I'm a bit reserved and don't show my emotions that often. I love the English climate and the English countryside. For my holiday, give me a deckchair on the beach and a hanky on my head and I'm happy. You know the sort of thing.

Some people wear their hearts on their sleeve, cry at the first mushy moment in a rom-com, process every small event in their lives in a loud and external way. But not me. Steady, quiet, not easily shaken. I don't have some oppressive family upbringing that has crushed me, I haven't got some heinous sin that I am struggling with. I haven't been emotionally stunted by the rejection of a series of girlfriends in my teens. It's just the way I am wired.

A bit boring, probably.

So as we worshipped away that evening, as I got the sense that God was demanding something of me that was out of my comfort zone, I felt – well, uncomfortable. Seriously uncomfortable.

But there was no doubt about it.

I needed to learn to dance.

Later that evening I was with the band and we were having a beer and slipping into that sort of tired, humorous banter that happens at such times. I started to explain what I had sensed that evening.

Now, for some reason, in life I tend to attract more than my fair share of ribbing. My staff meetings with my team at church invariably end up being a weekly "let's poke fun at Bennetts" hour. I'm a sort of office whipping-boy. When all else fails, let's have a joke at Bennetts' expense! Having a bad day? Why not pick on Bennetts? So in this moment, when I was baring my soul before my friends, it really didn't come as a surprise, although I do have to say publicly that I have since forgiven them for describing my dancing attempts as akin to "the embarrassing dad at the school disco".

To be fair, they did try to help.

They even began to suggest a few moves to me. One was called "stacking the shelves". Another was called "pulling in the fishing line". But while I appreciated their input, after a period of prayerful reflection I decided that those particular moves were not going to be appropriate for corporate worship. So, disappointed by the lack of sensible theological discussion with my friends, I decided the best approach was to do some more individual study on the matter.

Unsurprisingly, I turned to the life of David:

So David went down and brought up the ark of God
from the house of Obed-Edom to the City of David
with rejoicing. When those who were carrying the ark
of the Lord had taken six steps, he sacrificed a bull and
a fattened calf. David, wearing a linen ephod, danced

before the Lord with all his might, while he and the
entire house of Israel brought up the ark of the Lord
with shouts and the sound of trumpets.[214]

Of course, we have looked at the events leading up to this
passage in a previous chapter. Here we look at the worship that
surrounded the more successful journey of the ark to Jerusalem.

Getting up on the high wire: Facing our fears

I often find my heart resonating when I read the stories of
David. Now I'm not saying that I have fought giants, slept with
my neighbour's wife and then got her husband killed, or had
my songs published in the world's best-selling book. I've never
looked after sheep, I've never been chosen above my brothers
to be king over a whole nation, or spent a large amount of my
life being pursued by a madman and his army intent on killing
me. However, I do totally resonate with the way that throughout
his life, David had a huge desire to see the Name of God and the
honour of God and the glory of God upheld amongst the people
of God.

Now that's not a bad desire to have. Maybe, like me,
David's desire resonates with you as you look across much of
the church today. However, when it comes to the passion and
fervour that David displayed in worship, I sense my heart not so
much resonating, as being challenged. I find that David's overt,
intentional, visible act of undignified worship challenges my
Englishness and finds it wanting.

Let's face it, even the word "dance" leaves many of us breaking
out in a cold sweat.

We look at this dance of David and immediately try to
deflect the challenge it is to us. We say that worship is primarily
an activity of the heart – and of course it is. We say that we

214 2 Samuel 6:12–15.

can worship just as well sitting down quietly with head gently bowed – and of course we can. We say that we don't want to be exhibitionists and so prefer something a bit more reserved – and that may also be a good thing. But I wonder if all too often we duck down behind the wall when it comes to passion in worship because we don't grasp the heart of this story – the main thing that David is teaching us here.

The heart of this story is cost.

Or as David puts it elsewhere: "I will not sacrifice to the Lord my God burnt offerings that cost me nothing."[215]

David is teaching us here primarily about cost.

Sacrifice.

And what does cost, or sacrifice mean?

It means the letting go of something that was previously owned, held on to, treasured or valued.

When I worship passionately, I let go of my desire for self-determination and express reliance on God – and that costs me. When I worship passionately I physically spend energy and time on God that I could spend elsewhere – and that costs me. When I choose to spend time standing alongside other people singing songs, I let go of my independence and admit that I need others to help me on the journey – and that costs me. When I choose to come to church and sing when all around me is falling apart, I admit that there is Someone who is greater than I am and who knows better than I do and who can do a better job with my life than I can – and that costs me. When I choose to retreat to a mountain place and sit and pray and set my heart on God when there are a thousand good things I need to be doing, I let go of my need to impress people with my activity – and that costs me.

So the person who is tone deaf and yet chooses to stand and sing with those around him, even though his voice can't pitch the tune, is passionate. The person who still comes to church to worship even though they can't stand the noise of the band, is passionate. The person who engages with the actions of the kids'

---

215 2 Samuel 24:24.

songs even though they hate action songs, is passionate. The person who lays flat out on the floor in adoration even though they are aware of the questioning eyes of the worshippers around them, is passionate.

As I write this, I have just got back from our family holiday. We stayed on a campsite in France, and one of the activities provided was a high wire that weaved its way through the trees in the forest where the campsite was located, culminating in a long stretch of wire that went over the swimming pool, where bathers took great delight in chucking water up at those high-wiring above them. Not my idea of fun – but my girls were desperate to go on the wire. And so we booked them – only to find that they would only be allowed to go on it if an adult went with them.

And of course that meant me.

I hate heights.

In fact, whilst we're on the subject, I hate depths too.

One of my worst ministry trips was in another part of the UK where we were leading worship at a conference, and on the day off the rest of the team wanted to go to a place called the Heights of Abraham. It involved going high across a valley in a cable car, followed by a walk through the caverns under the hills in Derbyshire.

My basic nightmare.

I was traumatized.

And ridiculed because of it.

The memory of it is burnt deep within my heart.

And now here I was, on my family holiday, having the adventurist expectations of my children resting upon my height-fearing, depth-hating shoulders.

Of course I had to do it – but it did cost me. For a few minutes I had to move out of my comfort zone. Face my fears. Do something that doesn't come naturally. Do something I really didn't want to do. Unsurprisingly, I survived – even though I was sorely tempted to go and thump the person who chucked water over me as I flew high over the swimming pool, hanging on for dear life, to let them know exactly what I thought of them and the way they added to my discomfort.

Worship is passionate because it is costly. Worship is passionate because it involves sacrifice. If we want to dance, we need to be prepared to give something up that we have previously owned, held on to, treasured or valued.

Spend ourselves a little bit more.

Face our fears and get up on to the high wire.

A glorious obsession with the goodness of God: Celebrating God's goodness

In the moment that the Temple was filled with the glory of God, the priests fell on their faces and declared that God was good and that His love endured forever.[216] In that moment everything stopped. They were unable to do anything else other than fall down and acknowledge His goodness.[217]

It seems deeply embedded within our culture to look for the bad, the ugly, the sad, the lonely, the deprived, the broken, and the desperately unfair in everything. Just look at TV these days. Storylines deal with the depressed and the addicted and the insecure and unfulfilled. Whether its *Watchdog* which looks for the powerful manipulator, *Eastenders* which looks for the tragic infidel, *Supernanny* which looks for the struggling parent, or *Kitchen Nightmares* which looks for the most unhealthy and unimaginative cook in the country.

Or look at the news items that come our way every day. It seems the only good story is a bad story. It all points to an unhealthy obsession with bad news. Even when a seemingly good news story breaks, we are suspicious of it. There is a huge effort and investigation that seems to swing into action that seeks to deny it. Find the corruption underlying it. Find the people

216 2 Chronicles 5:13.
217 2 Chronicles 5:14.

making money out of it. Rob it of its power.

It is into all of this that the church stands and shouts its rebellious refrain: "God is Good!"

In the same way that, as the ark is being transported to Jerusalem, the people of God are rejoicing, and celebrating, so the church should be a place that declares and celebrates the good things of God. Celebrating goodness should be one of our primary calling cards. Not that we don't weep with those that weep – of course we do – and when we do, we do it with as much hope and faith as possible. But it seems to me that the church is more comfortable with weeping than with celebrating, and maybe we need to learn to do both equally well.

As a worship leader I know that the hardest thing to lead my church in is high praise. As a songwriter, I find it far harder to write a song of celebration and energy, and this seems pretty usual for the worship leaders and songwriters I know. When a good new "fast" song is written, we all grab it and use it as much as we can – and probably overuse it.

Maybe the church needs to grow in this. Maybe we need to become better at celebrating and rejoicing. Maybe we need to counter our culture's unhealthy obsession with misery with a glorious obsession with the goodness of God. Maybe if we did that, we would find we had more to dance about than we thought.

Digging for diamonds: Going deeper with God in His word

It is so easy in life to get desensitized to great things – to get used to the mediocre.

I like to write songs to sing in church. When I get stuck, one of the things I am tempted to do is flick through the Psalms to try to get a quick fix – a line or word or expression that gets me the rhyme or set of words that fits the gap I have been struggling to fill. Or I scan a few old hymns in one of the old hymn-books I have lying around in the hope that I can nick someone else's idea without the danger of being sued. By the grace of God sometimes this works, but if I am going to be honest, it is normally pretty fruitless.

After one particularly dry season of song-writing when I became particularly frustrated by my lack of creativity and productivity, I felt the Lord drop a little phrase into my heart. I felt Him say that I needed to start digging for diamonds, that I needed to go much, much deeper with Him and in His word before I came back up to the surface and asked my church to sing what I had written. I realized that in many ways I had been scratching the surface too much – and like any surface that gets continually scratched, it eventually just becomes dull. A bit like my song-writing at that point, to be honest.

I rarely meet a worship leader these days who doesn't love the presence of God, or who doesn't know that there is a link between worship and justice or pursue creativity or use various bits of Apple software or know the background to the production on the latest worship album.

However, I wonder how many of those of us who lead and influence worship in our churches today have a really well-formed and deep theological framework from which to operate. Not a crusty, dour, pompous, removed-from-this-world-intellectualism type of theological framework, but a freedom-bringing, eye-opening, whole-truth, life-enhancing, energy-sparking type of theological framework. One that can only come from a diamond-digging sort of attitude.

Is it just me, or do you also find that when the word of God is preached faithfully, creatively, and with no embarrassment, you feel inspired to sing a bit more in response? I am all for culturally relevant, creative, thought-provoking opinion, but what really brings my spirit alive is a Spirit-filled journey down into the depths of the Scriptures.

A generous and persistent application: Being prepared to work hard

Our lead Pastor Mark Bailey has a mantra that permeates throughout our church life and it is this: we should pray like it depends on God, and work like it depends on ourselves. David was clearly a prayerful person, but he also would have had to be a very hard worker – a carnival and journey on this scale wouldn't have just happened on its own.

I think that most of us get the prayer bit – what we seem to struggle with, though, is the work bit. In my experience it is always clear which members of your staff team have spent a significant period of time working in a secular business environment. They, more often than not, have a work ethic that carries them through. Often, worship leaders who have never had to survive in the harsh reality of full-time non-church employment will be disorganized, poor communicators, and poor people managers. They will tend to be people who sit around waiting for the anointing to fall rather than running the race with all of the energy and purposeful diligence that that requires.

I remember, many years ago, playing in a band for a worship leader at some event. We came to one song, and I asked him what the introduction for the song was. He turned to me and said, "We don't do introductions here – we just worship." Now of course, I understand where he was coming from, but it does seem to me that all too often we expect worship to just happen without us working hard at it. From my experience, freedom and fluid, Spirit-led worship tend to come off the back of hard work and diligent preparation just as much as a prayerful attitude.

I even think that even though creativity itself may have its origins in a whisper from God, it tends to find its fruitfulness in our generous and persistent application.

Kathryn Scott tells me that when she wrote the song "Hungry", she actually wrote it many, many times over a period of months. Brian Doerksen was mentoring her through that time, and he kept sending her away to work at it again. I'm quite glad that he asked her to do it, and glad that Kathryn did, because we are left with a diamond song.

Hard work doesn't deny the inspiration of God.

In fact, I think it confirms it.

Rejoicing in the success of others: Letting others fly

Jay Pathak, the lead pastor of the Arvada Vineyard, recently said this: "What is that thing called when you let others do the things that you yourself used to really enjoy doing?... Oh yes... it's called growing up!"

I remember many years ago, when I first started getting involved in New Wine, I sensed the Lord say to me that the reason I was there was to give away a platform to other worship leaders. So for that reason, as far as has been possible, I have always asked new people to lead alongside me, and always tried to rejoice in their success.

One of the first years I did this, I stood worshipping away on the front row as this younger worship leader led worship on stage, and I had some thoughts that went something like this: "This worship is going well... very well... and I'm not even on the stage... I hoped it would be good... but I never thought it would be this good."

Inside of me my heart was burning a little... dare I say it... with a little insecure jealousy. As I struggled with my feelings on that evening, I sensed the Lord say to me, "Well, you said you wanted to raise others up... Well, if you really commit to that, then there will be many more evenings like this one."

Ouch.

The truth is that if we truly want to rejoice in the success of others, we need to be prepared not only to let them do what we ourselves enjoy doing, but equally we need to be prepared for the fact that no one may even acknowledge that we had anything to do with their success.

I remember a Christmas celebration we did recently in our church. We hired out the biggest venue in Cheltenham and put on an amazing carol service – we had great lights and effects, a great band with ten drummers, great video reading and footage, and some amazing arrangements of carols, and a great talk from my friend Mark Bailey. And for this one year I even got to play a grand piano that we hired in for the event. It was a great evening, with many guests from around the town. Maybe a little bit flushed with success, when I got home, I asked my daughters what they enjoyed the most, hoping to bask in their daughterly adoration. First they said, "Mark's talk." Then they said a solo by one of the singers.

The list went on.

They didn't even mention my piano playing.

I didn't get a look in!

Leadership is often like that. You think you achieve something amazing, and for some reason you don't even get a whisper of recognition.

We need to be prepared for it. Or as Harry Truman once said, "It's amazing what you can achieve in life if you don't mind who gets the credit."

I reckon that as I get on in years, the main thing that will justify my continued place as a senior worship pastor will be the extent to which I release others to fly. Too often churches get stuck in a rut because people who have done great things fail to let others have a go.

Like the rich man whose money weighed so heavily on him that he wasn't able to follow Jesus, we too can become so preoccupied with our own ministry that it weighs the church down, stifles it, and stops it dancing.

Going the way of the best: Excellence in worship

It seems totally incomprehensible to me that anyone would give anything other than their best in their worship of God, and yet there seems to have been endless debate on the issue of church and worship and a pursuit of excellence.

Excellence, to me, is an attitude, not a standard. It is an attitude of doing the absolute best with what God entrusts to you. Like in the parable of the talents, the important thing is not so much what you are given by God; it is what you do with what you are given. There is not some predefined standard that any church needs to aspire to before its worship becomes acceptable. That is perfectionism, and we should avoid it at all costs, as it can quickly become crushing for the people and churches we lead. But we can, and should, always aspire to doing our best.

There have been a few themes that have run through my life and my ministry. One of those themes is this theme of excellence – in its widest application. It is inbuilt in me to try to do things well. And over many years that has meant that I have had to deal with accusations of extravagance. This rears its head in many forms. It may come because I need to spend certain amounts of money so that our worship sounds good in church on Sunday. It may come because I insist that we get enough people on stage in the band to give it a great sound. It may be because I spend far too long working at a few bars in a song I am writing until it gets as good as possible. Sometimes these accusations are light-hearted. Often they are not. And occasionally they hurt – but not too much these days because I have learned to expect them and have learned how to respond. But in my mind the church has suffered more down the ages because of its stinginess in worship than it has through its extravagance in worship. It has suffered far more because of laxity and laziness and the pursuit of the average than through hard work and generous application. That's why, for me, if there is ever a choice, I will continue to choose extravagance. I will continue to pursue excellence. I will continue to go the way of the best.

When the rubber hits the road: Being prepared to pay for it

"Fame costs. And this is where you start paying – in sweat."

These are the historic words that introduced every episode of the hit show *Fame* that I watched as I was growing up. Well, at the risk of sounding a little cheesy, maybe we in our churches should have our own mantra: "Worship costs. And this is where we start paying – in cash."

When the proverbial rubber hits the road in church life, the question we will inevitably have to answer at some point is this: are we prepared to pay for it?

As the ark is being transported to Jerusalem, every six steps they all stopped and David sacrificed a bull and a fattened calf.[218] Now I don't know the whole length of the journey, and opinion is divided on whether these sacrifices happened literally every six steps, but whatever angle you come from, this was a whole truckload of meat. And my guess is that this wasn't the poor-quality stuff. It wasn't the old or lame or diseased, it was the young and the fit and the healthy.

No, this offering wasn't cheap.

It was the very, very best that was on offer.

I suspect the cost of those sacrifices in purely financial terms would have brought water to the eyes of any finance director or accountant. I certainly would have struggled to get it agreed on my church worship budget. Of course, you could argue that David was the King, that this was an event of national importance, and so the money "just had to be available", and so any such comparison with most of us in local church life is unfair. And there is probably some truth in that. But I am also

---

218 2 Samuel 6:13.

often slightly confused when I look around many churches and find that, alongside what seems to be a huge desire to grow in worship, there is a great reluctance to spend any money on it. I know we need to be wise. I know we have to balance the cost of PA systems and worship leaders with the cost of serving the poor. I know, I know, I know. But given that our first priority is to worship God (and that is the worship-as-we-sing-our-songs worship as well as the worship-as-a-lifestyle worship), I question whether this gets properly and wisely translated into the balance sheet of many of our churches.

Worship should be the core family value of any church. Before anything else, every church should turn its attention on to its gathered worship, because it is from this place that everything else grows and flourishes. I have been so fortunate to be part of a church that understands this, and particularly understands the costs associated with worship. Because the fact is that worship doesn't come cheap and whereas our individual circumstances and local church settings may all be different, at some point, that cost will almost inevitably mean hard cash.

I have, like many other people of my generation – especially worship leaders of my generation – been hugely impacted by John Wimber and the Vineyard church network that he founded and led. One of his passions – possibly his first passion – was worship and worship leaders. He was a huge personal encouragement to many of the worship leaders who have profoundly impacted the worshipping life of the worldwide church in recent years.

When the vineyard planted a church, they sent a pastor, a worship leader and a PA system. A pastor to preach the word and lead the church, a worship leader to lead the worship, and a PA system so that the congregation could hear what they were both doing.

Everything else was built from there.

Investment in worship came right at the beginning. Even for staffing. Compare that with most churches where a paid worship leader will probably be way down the list of priorities – if it is there at all.

Some people wince when I talk about gathered worship being the first priority of the church. You may be one of them. But let me encourage you to think about it like this: the most important thing for a church to be doing is the thing that will cause it to fall apart the most quickly if it is stopped.

Sounds like worship to me.

An infectious lack of dignity: Passionate worship that attracts the attention of the world

I once played drums in our church.

Actually, I can't really play drums, it's just that no one else was there and I could hold a beat and thought I would try to model great servant leadership for people and play along with another worship leader. He did that Matt Redman song "Undignified".

I have to confess I don't love the song, but I do love its message and so went with it.

This was in the early days in our time at Trinity Cheltenham, and we were still fighting many battles on the worship front, and so whether or not this was the wisest time to introduce one of the edgiest songs of that time into our Sunday morning worship, I am not sure – but we did it all the same.

It was a warm summer morning, and after the service I was saying goodbye to some people outside the church when I was approached by one of our more generally disgruntled members, dressed in shorts and sandals (no socks). He took me to one side and laid into me about the song, and particularly how he didn't think we should be undignified. He said that if I ever did that song in church again, he would get up and walk out.

Then having delivered what he clearly thought was a crushing blow in a pleasingly fitting manner, he turned his back, strode off purposefully and promptly stepped into an enormous dog poo that had been deposited on the pathway.

Remember, he was wearing open sandals with no socks.

My lasting impression was of this chap trying to walk away purposefully and angrily while at the same time trying to shake away this dog poo that had mashed itself around his foot and between his un-socked toes.

It seemed to me that despite his best efforts, he had become undignified after all.

OK, so that story won't win me any favours with those of you of a weak disposition, but the truth is that many of us don't like the sound of losing our dignity in worship, because above all, we fear that it will lose us credibility with our friends, neighbours or communities.

However, it seems to me that rather than alienate people, undignified worship is infectious. It's infectious to the people in church around us and it's also infectious to the people outside the church. In a church culture where so many people talk about being seeker friendly as the motivation for softening their expression of worship, I sometimes want to pull my hair out and scream (actually, I don't have much hair... but if I did, I would definitely be trying to pull it out), because it seems to me that the most attractive, attention-grabbing, thought-provoking, heart-stirring thing that the world can see is the church immersing themselves in the passionate, extravagant, authentic worship of God.

You see, if we produce great visuals, or great drama presentations, or great song performances, we may well cause people's eyes to glance in our direction – which is important in itself – but when we also engage in a passionate, worshipful encounter with God, we will also cause their hearts to be stirred to the things of His Kingdom. Wasn't it amidst the messy environment of a prophetic Corinthian church that the outsider fell on his knees and declared, "God is really among you"?[219]

---

219 1 Corinthians 14:25.

Over my years in worship ministry I have led worship at many weddings. So often the church is made up of two main groups of people. Firstly the Christians, who love the worship, lift their hands and go for it. Then secondly there are those who have hardly, if ever, been to church or explored a relationship with God. They tend to stand during the songs and look totally confused by what is unfolding before them. So often, though, in the conversations that you have with people after the service, it is the worship that they remember. It is the worship that they have decided to dwell on. Their hearts have been stirred to the things of God.

Because passionate worship is infectious.

I recently went to Paris with my family, and we went into the Sacré Coeur. It is a beautiful church. The day we went in, there was actually a service going on. Part of the church was roped off, and visitors – suitably instructed to keep quiet – were allowed to wander around the outer parts of the church building while the worship was going on in the middle of the building. At first I thought that it was a shame that the tourists were allowed in while the worship was going on – it felt slightly irreverent to me. But then I noticed something. People would stop, look, and start taking pictures of the worship. They were intrigued by what was going on.

I wonder what the impact would be if we filled the great cathedrals of our country with Spirit-filled, passionate worshippers. We wouldn't even need to invite guests – they already flood round these buildings in their thousands. What an opportunity that presents, because I am convinced that a dancing church is a missional church. As John Piper says:

Missions is not the ultimate goal of the church.
Worship is. Mission exists because worship doesn't.
Worship is ultimate, not missions, because God is
ultimate, not man. When this age is over, and the
countless millions of the redeemed fall on their faces

before the throne of God, missions will be no more. It is a temporary necessity. But worship abides forever. Worship, therefore, is the fuel and goal of missions. It's the goal of missions because in missions we simply aim to bring the nations into the white-hot enjoyment of God's glory. The goal of missions is the gladness of the peoples in the greatness of God.[220]

Worship is about what God is worth, not what we feel able to give

David, dressed in his ceremonial outfit, danced before the Lord with all his might.[221]

One thing is clear: this was a very personal, passionate display of one man's love of God. He laid aside all normal dignity, and went for it, but that was only the start. We read that the "whole house of Israel" was with him.[222] Personal and passionate it may have been. Private it certainly wasn't. David was modelling worship to the entire nation that day. He was saying, "This is what God is worth, this is the type of worship that delights God's heart."

Here is the man who was chosen because "People look at the outward appearance, but the Lord looks at the heart."[223] He was engaging in an act of worship that every person around was going to see. It seems that the worship that started in his heart, just had to find a way out.

The Hebrew word translated as "dance" in this passage is *karar*[224] – which essentially means to whirl around. The other word used is *pazaz*,[225] which essentially means leaping.

David the shepherd-boy-come-king danced, and as he

---

220 *Let the Nations Be Glad*, IVP, 2004, p. 17.
221 2 Samuel 6:14.
222 2 Samuel 6:5
223 1 Samuel 16:7.
224 2 Samuel 6:14.
225 1 Chronicles 15:29.

danced he spun around and leapt in the air. David was not a weirdo on the fringes. He wasn't a slightly mad, whacky type. He was the King of Israel. The most important character amongst the people of God, showing them how to worship.

By spinning around and leaping high!

All other reserved, introverted Englishmen join with me in expressions of abject horror!

I don't know if you've heard this sort of comment from worshippers: "It's just so important that I'm true to myself when I worship, that I should just be me, little old me." Well, part of me wants to say "yes". But actually, I know I need to say "no".

Worship has never been about what we want to give, but it has always been about what God is worth. And God requires extravagant, expensive, risky, costly, sacrificial worship.

Whether I feel like it or not.

David, in Psalm 57, echoes this:

My heart is steadfast, O God, my heart is steadfast;
I will sing and make music. Awake, my soul! Awake,
harp and lyre! I will awaken the dawn.[226]

Sometimes it doesn't come naturally. Sometime our souls feel weak, and we need to wake them. Sometimes the last thing our feet feel like doing is dancing and we need to purposefully step out. Sometimes we don't feel like singing but we need to intentionally stir within us a desire to open our mouths. Sometimes we just need to be intentionally passionate.

A few years ago, when all of this dawned on me, I started to try to put a lot of this in practice. At that time one of my great friends, Naomi Lippett, was working with me at our church, and I remember her coming up to me one day and saying something like, "We're seeing some passion in your worship that seems out of your normal character. It's great to see, mate – keep going!" It sounded strange at the time – but actually I

---

226 Psalm 57:7–8.

took that as a compliment.

However, I still haven't mustered up the courage to spin around and leap in the air. But I think I am on a journey with this, and maybe one day I will!

A church that dances

Don't you long for the church in this country to be one that is dancing? I get so depressed when I see so many people and churches where any sense of passion and adventure and excitement in worship has been lost – where worship is something to be endured rather than relished. Worse than that, the more I think about it, the more I think that people – both inside and outside the church – don't even know that there is a dance to be danced.

I remember a party at church a few years ago. I can't remember exactly what it was, but I know the rest of the leadership team was there, and I also remember that, during the family disco at the end of the evening, my eldest daughter – I think she was about nine at the time – was being particularly exuberant in her dance-floor antics.

I was standing watching her throw herself around – obviously attracting a fair bit of attention – and I remember wondering what it would be like to have a daughter who was more refined, temperate and sophisticated at such events. I could almost sense the whispered comments from others around me (of course, there were no such comments outside of my imagination). Then my daughter came up to me – hot and excited and even fuller of energy than I felt possible, and she encouraged me to join her.

My first reaction was not positive.

Then something clicked inside of me.

Here was my amazing daughter, full of life and energy and sparkle, asking me to be part of what she was doing.

All she wanted was for me to dance with her.

How could I possibly refuse?

One description of God – the triune Father, Son, and Holy Spirit – is "Circle Dance".

When God invites us into a dance, He is asking us to join in what He already does, and enjoys, and experiences. Something that is the essence of reality and wonder and life itself.

Let us be sure, there is a dance to be danced, and God is asking us to join Him in it.

So, come on, church.

Let's dance!

Chapter 12

Now to Him

DOXOLOGY

Simon Ponsonby

Now to him who is able to keep you from stumbling and to present you blameless before the presence of his glory with great joy, to the only God, our Saviour, through Jesus Christ our Lord, be glory, majesty, dominion, and authority, before all time and now and forever. Amen.[227]

Jude is one of only three letters in the New Testament (the others being Romans and 2 Peter) which end with worship. Most of the epistles end with exhortations, personal comments, or blessings, but Jude closes on a high note of praise, with a doxology (from the Greek word *doxa*, which means "glory"), glorifying God. This is not because worship is the last thing on Jude's list, the tag end, but because it's the most important, the climax, the conclusion of all things.

Whatever else needs saying, whatever doctrines need reaffirming, whatever pastoral measures need establishing, we finish with worship.

There are many who begin their Christian life with worship and praise, the early days swelling with thanksgiving and rejoicing at finding God, receiving forgiveness. But the exigencies, temptations, even disappointments of life can wear down that initial rush of passion and weather out their worship.

---

227 Jude 24–25.

We can lose that sense of wonder in God, the desire to adore and enjoy Jesus. And when passion for worship ceases, we become grumpy old men and women. The writer of the letter to the Hebrews encourages us to be like the patriarch Jacob, who when dying, "By faith... blessed each of the sons of Joseph, bowing in worship over the head of his staff" (11:21). How wonderful it would be to seamlessly leave this world whilst worshipping, to enter heaven worshipping.

Worship is to God

Jude finishes his corrective letter with the words, "Now – to him".

The church often gets abstracted from her central purpose. But Jude refocuses them – now, right now, not tomorrow, not next Sunday, not next summer conference, not when you next feel like it, but now, is the time to turn to God in worship. The command of God to orientate a life in worship to God always confronts us in the now. It is the ever-present now. When to him? Now! When do I give God glory? Now.

If the time is "now", the orientation is "to Him". It is very often the case that we worship worship rather than worship God. Jude introduces both concluding sentences with the subject of our glorying: "to Him, to God". It's to Him, to God – He is the object and subject of worship, He is the direction of our affections, He is the focus of our devotions. It's about Him, it's because of Him, it's to Him. One of the causes of the crisis in the churches which Jude is addressing is that the members had been deceived into thinking it was all about them, their needs, their desires, their enjoyment, rather than being all about *God*. And consequently, they had been duped, deceived by false teachers offering false spiritual experiences, teaching false doctrine. The great safeguard to deception and deviation from the faith is recognizing and dwelling in the "now, to Him". The psalmist understood this as he worshipped: "Not to us, O Lord, not to us, but to your name give glory, for the sake of your steadfast love and your faithfulness!"[228] This worship and praise is now to Him, it's not to us.

I am concerned at the hedonistic, introspective, self-satisfying influences in much of church life today – as if church is about us and for us. Not often is God the great obsession and preoccupation of today's saints. One regularly hears questions like: "How was the worship?" And responses like: "Oh, too long, too short, too loud, too quiet, too many songs," etc.

As a young Christian, I remember talking with someone about a service. I criticized: "I didn't think much of that worship", and immediately God's Spirit spoke to my soul and said, "I did." We aren't the point of worship – our enjoyment is irrelevant. It's to Him. We are to bring a sacrifice of praise; true worship is costly, not cosy. We should leave church exhausted but satisfied – our emotions and intellects spent on worship and engagement with God.

Worship is not about style, liturgy, volume, instrumentation – these things are less than secondary. What matters is whether it's "to Him – unto God". True worship, worship in spirit and truth, "the beautiful thing" Jesus looks for, may be expressed in Gregorian chant, Bach's choral music, Wesleyan hymns, intimate worship songs, driving plugged-in anthems – that is all personal preference. God always looks at our heart to see whether He is there.

Worship is not an evangelistic tool – because it is "to Him", it is not "to us".

Historically, D. L. Moody with the singer Ira Sankey and Billy Graham with the singer Beverly Shea used worship hymns, sung to contemporary tunes, as an evangelistic aid. In the 1980s we had so-called "Rock Masses" and in the 1990s "Raves in the Nave". In the twenty-first century we have ambient religious music in café settings. Now, while there is nothing wrong per se in trying to place worship in a musical medium which is accessible to a specific generation or culture, which may help rather than

---

228 Psalm 115:1.

hinder their responding to God, we must not think it in itself is evangelism – the focus is not and never should be the non-Christian, or the Christian. Worship is for God, His glory, His enjoyment. Neither worshippers nor seekers set the agenda for worship. The One who is sought does. If we invert this and think our appetites set the agenda, we are very close to idolatry.

If we don't worship God, we will worship something else, for man is made to worship. If worship is not given "to Him" (and I suspect that not infrequently in church something other than God is at the heart of our worship), then we worship idols.

Worship "to God" discloses something of who God is

When the disciples saw the Temple stones in Jerusalem, each the size of a barn, they were impressed: "Wow! Look, teacher, what massive stones, what an amazing building" (see Mark 13:1). That's rather sad. They were impressed by the container and context of worship, rather than the God worshipped. The disciples were awed at the masons' handiwork rather than the majesty of God whose name was associated with this place, whose forgiveness was mediated here through sacrifices for sin. How many times have people been moved by the magnificence of the grand architectonic structure of an English cathedral, without a thought for the God to whom it was dedicated? Well, Jude shows us not massive temple stones to arouse awe, but massive attributes of God which provoke true worship.

Incomparable

First, we worship the God who is incomparable: "to the only God [Greek: *mono-theo*], our Saviour, through Jesus Christ our Lord, be glory, majesty, dominion and authority."[229]

Prince Charles, the Prince of Wales, holds numerous titles and honours. Among the less well known are Ojibway (which

---

229 Jude 25.

means "The sun looks at him in a good way") of Saskatchewan; Colonel in Chief of the British Army; Air Commodore of the Royal Air Force; Admiral of the British Navy; Honorary DLitt; Dr Civil Law; Dr Music; Knight of the Order of the Bath; Knight of the Order of the Garter; Knight of the Order of the Elephant. Pretty impressive, but, with respect, generally speaking his titles come with the job of being born heir apparent to the throne of England, a privileged birth rather than any inherent merit. His degrees are unearned, his military offices honorary, not functional.

But God's titles are His by right. He is the only God because there is no other. He is the Saviour because He alone could save. He is the personification of glory, majesty, authority. He can neither increase nor decrease – they are His DNA, His being, His nature, Him. In St John's vision of heaven in the book of Revelation, he sees angels and martyrs round the throne worshipping the incomparable Creator and Saviour: "Worthy are you, our Lord and God, to receive glory and honor and power, for you created all things, and by your will they existed and were created";[230] "Worthy are you to take the scroll and to open its seals [control history], for you were slain, and by your blood you ransomed people for God".[231]

Jude offers a doxology – giving glory to God. If we don't give God glory we don't in any way diminish His glory, we simply diminish ourselves. As C. S. Lewis rightly quipped: "man can no more diminish God's glory by refusing to worship Him than a lunatic can put out the sun by scribbling the word, 'darkness' on the walls of his cell."[232] To give glory to God is to recognize His glory and give ourselves to Him and participate in His glory.

230 Revelation 4:11.
231 Revelation 5:9.
232 C. S. Lewis, *The Problem of Pain*, Harper Collins, 1940, p. 41.

Personal

Second, we worship the God who is personal.

Twice Jude says God is "ours": "our Saviour", "our Lord".[233]

Ours is not the distant divine of the Deists, who believe God wound up the world, set its laws in order, than abandoned us to ourselves. Neither is ours the indifferent god of the Greeks, who defined the nature of the gods as *apatheia* – indifferent and apathetic to the life of humankind, who are just pawns to move on earth's chessboard at their whim and for their pleasure. Nor is ours the malevolent god of paganism, violent and unpredictable, who needs appeasing or controlling through magic.

The God revealed in Scripture, revealed pre-eminently in the person and work of Jesus Christ, is a personal God who allows us to call Him not just *the* Lord, but *our* Lord, who gives Himself to us in love and who says: "I will be your God and you will be my people." And this is who and this is why we worship.

Christological

Third, we worship the God who is Christological: "through Jesus Christ our Lord".[234]

True worship is "through worship" – through Jesus Christ who is Lord. Worship which is not through Jesus, worship that does not have Jesus Christ as cause and conduit, is not the true worship which the Father requires and which He receives.

Jesus alone gives access to God. He alone is the sufficient sacrifice to take away the sins of the world and make us fit to draw near to God with clean hands. He alone is the great High Priest who goes into the sanctuary of the Father and sits down on our behalf. Though non-Christian worship may be sincere in its desire for God, if it is not mediated by the blood of Jesus, in the Spirit of Jesus, through faith in Jesus, then it is not worship of God as God requires. Bart Simpson sarcastically states, "Christmas is a time when people of all religions come together

---

233 Jude 25.
234 Jude 25.

to worship Jesus Christ." Of course, this is not the case – but one day, every knee will bow and every tongue will confess what we Christians know now – that Jesus is Lord.

Eternal

Fourth, we worship the God who is eternal: "before all time, now and forever."[235]

We worship the God who was, is and is to come. Our worship here in time and space, on planet earth, in the twenty-first century, in our church or kitchen or study or bedroom, is worship which joins with all other worship of God flowing from before time and flowing into eternity.

Worship is an eternal event: it transcends time, touching prehistory with the worship of God by legions of angels before God spoke the world into being. It is an eschatological event that unites us to the end of time when time is wrapped up and we are gathered around the eternal throne, enjoying God for ever.

Worship is a response to what God has done for us

Worship is elicited freely and fully when we grasp who God is and what God has done for us. Richard Foster wrote: "Worship is our response to the overtures of love from the heart of the Father."[236]

Jude here highlights four great overtures from the heart of God:

God has saved us

First, God has saved us: He is "our Saviour" (Greek: *soter*) – rescuer, deliverer, preserver. We don't save ourselves, we can't. Christ, the Good Shepherd, came to seek and save the lost. He found us, we didn't find Him; he fought off our enemies of death and the demonic and brought us home. He was the Good

---

235 Jude 25.
236 Richard Foster, *Celebration of Discipline*, Harper Collins, 1978, p. 158.

Samaritan who bandaged our wounds from robbers, placed us in an inn, paid for our care, promised to return.

As a child I often played "Swap" – my penknife for your skateboard; my Top Trumps for your football cards. Jesus came and offered a swap. He took our punishment and we took His peace; He took our sinfulness and we took His righteousness; He took our forsakenness and we took His sonship; He took our death and we took His life; He took our hell and we took His heaven. It was not a fair swap – heaven's glory for Golgotha's gallows – but He did it freely, willingly, joyfully because He loved us.

God has sustained us

Second, God has sustained us: "He is able [literally, 'has power', *dunami*] to keep you [literally, 'guard you'] from falling."

He will not let us fall (Greek verb *ptaio*, used of a sure-footed horse). Like a parent who holds the hands of their toddler as they learn to walk, ready to hold and catch them if they stumble, so the Lord holds and leads us. Yes, we can pull away, loose His hold on us and run away into danger, but whilst we willingly hold up our hands to be held and led, we are safe and secure.

The notion that God is able to keep us from falling may at first glance seem a strange lead into worship. Is that the basis of our glorying God? Why did Jude emphasize this? Well, speaking personally, God's faithfulness in sustaining me has become a real cause for my delight and gratitude to Him.

Some years ago I was in a very dark place. I was on heart tablets which I later learnt had serious side-effects and were well known for causing severe depression in 10 per cent of users. I was not aware of these medical side-effects, but it seemed all hell was let loose on me and in my mind. God seemed a distant memory, I was filled with irrational and bizarre thoughts. Hopelessness and despair mounted until suicidal thoughts began to gather like ominous clouds and death seemed a deliverance.

One night, walking near the coast, waves were crashing and seemingly inviting me in to end the pain.

I was tempted.

Then suddenly God thundered this very verse from Jude into my mind: "he is able to keep you from falling". And I swear, the clouds seemed to part, the moonlight shone on me, comfort surrounded me. I was kept from falling.

Just a few weeks later I was talking to a fellow minister when I asked the customary, "How are you?"

He immediately replied: "I'm OK now, but I have been severely depressed due to my heart medications, which I've now changed."

I couldn't believe what I was hearing. I asked: "What heart tablets were you on that caused your depression?"

I shouldn't have been surprised – he had been on exactly the same medication and exactly the same dose as me. I immediately made an appointment with my doctor, and within forty-eight hours I was off those meds, and out of the shadows. God stood with me and kept me from falling within the storm, and then freed me completely from the source. As I reflect on this dark experience and God's deliverance, I am filled with wonder and worship. Yes, God can and does and will keep me from falling.

God has sanctified us

Third, God has sanctified us: "and present you faultless [Greek: *amomos*, used of a spotless offering] before his glorious sight."

When God brought the high priest Joshua before him (Zechariah 3), he was seen standing in filthy clothes. The presence and purity of God shows up all our stain. But God said, "I have taken away your sin, and I will put rich garments on you"[237] – then the angel clothed him. God robes us in His righteousness. What He commands He gives. He invites us to the wedding, and then gives us the wedding clothes. God presents us before

---

237 Zechariah 3:4 NIV.

His presence (the Greek actually says He presents us before His eyes), up close. God brings us before Himself, He clothes us so we may stand before Him acceptably.

If you achieve something in your profession, you may well get an audience with the Queen, where you receive an honour, an OBE, a CBE, a Knighthood, perhaps – but you have to achieve it (even if it means a generous donation to a political party!). If the honour is accepted, you go to your tailor or dressmaker and you get fitted and kitted and presented before the Queen on the basis of what you have merited or achieved. But God gets us ready for His glorious presence. He does all the work – He is the one who achieves something for us in Christ. He then fits and kits us for His presence; He brings us to Himself; He holds us and draws us and honours us.

God has satisfied us

Fourth, God has satisfied us: "with great joy".

We don't come fearfully, anxiously, wondering what our fate will be. We stand tall, before His eyes bathed in love, clothed in holy garments. And then literally, we jump for joy.

The term in Greek is *agalliasis*, and is unique in the New Testament; indeed, it is unknown in ancient secular Greek. Why would Jude invent a word to describe our response to God and His saving work? Because the joy that God gives is unique, without precedent. Only He can give this gift of joy. The word Jude creates is a conjunction of two root words – the word for a leaping, bubbling spring and the word for gladness, thus rendering a meaning which is literally, "jump for joy".

Worship involves rejoicing, a joyful, exuberant thanksgiving for who God is and what God has done. This is depicted in Bunyan's classic, *Pilgrim's Progress*, where Pilgrim (the symbol of a disciple) comes to the cross and his weighty rucksack is lifted off him (symbolizing the removal of sin), and he experiences true forgiveness. "He stood awhile to look and wonder... he looked again even until the springs that were in his head sent water down his cheeks. Then Christian gave three leaps for joy and went on singing."

The revelation of God's love, the experience of God's forgiveness, causes a geyser of joy to erupt in spontaneous, effervescent praise.

In conclusion

We have seen here in Jude's doxology the ever-present "Now" of worship "to Him, to God".

It is our inadequate response to God for who He is and for what He has done for us. But here is an amazing thing – the very thought of which should make us break out in praise and worship. Many years ago, the Prophet Zephaniah wrote: "The Lord your God is with you, he is mighty to save. He will take great delight in you... he will rejoice over you with singing."[238]

The one we delight in delights in us. The one we sing to in joy, sings over us joyfully. Wow!

---

238   Zephaniah 3:17 NIV.